FLAVORS OF CHATHAM

Reflections & Recipes

*A Centennial Celebration of
The Women's Club of Chatham*

McClafferty Printing Company
1600 North Scott Street
Wilmington, DE 19806
www.mcclaffertyprinting.com

Any inquires about this book or for additional copies contact:
The Women's Club of Chatham
P.O. Box 463
Chatham, MA 02633
www.womensclubofchatham.org

ISBN 978-0-692-29393-5

Copyright © 2014 by The Women's Club of Chatham

All rights reserved. No part of this publication may be reproduced or transmitted in any form by any means, electronic or mechanical, including photocopying, recording, or any other information storage and retrieval system, without written permission of the copyright owners.

A great effort has been made to ensure that the information in this book is accurate. However, there is the possibility of errors in this ambitious undertaking.

The Women's Club of Chatham
"Connecting Women ~ Enriching Community"

Founded in 1915 with forty-two charter members, The Women's Club of Chatham is now among the largest women's clubs in Massachusetts. In 2010 we withdrew from the General Federation of Women's Clubs and became an independent non-profit 501(c)(3) organization.

Our objective is to enrich the educational and civic lives of our members and the community. The Women's Club of Chatham is an organization for today's world that seeks to be meaningful in the lives of our members. While promoting our philanthropic, educational and civic involvement, we encourage friendship, fun and celebration.

Dedication

This book is dedicated to all the women who over the past one hundred years have been members of The Women's Club of Chatham. We honor their legacy. For present and future members it is a heritage that continues to create traditions, form friendships and enrich the community.

Expression of Appreciation

In one short year the fantastic women of The Women's Club of Chatham have taken the glimmer of an idea and created this wonderful book. The small group of women who first met to discuss the project has grown, divided into committees and engaged the members of the club to contribute. Eighty-seven members submitted art, reflections and/or recipes. Many more have worked on the production, editing, proofreading, layout, marketing, advertising and sales. This has truly been a entire club project. Our thanks to all our enthusiastic club members whose hard work made this book possible.

Front Cover Artist

Karen Schwalm began working with watercolor after she retired. During her career, she enjoyed working with commercial artists and photographers to create marketing materials. She is an active member of and has displayed her work at the Creative Arts Center of Chatham and the Cape Cod Art Association. She takes pleasure in living on the Cape, seeing the ever changing land and seascapes.

Back Cover Artist

Barbara Hamilton Gibson retired to Cape Cod in 2006 and immediately began to pursue her passion for watercolor. She is an active member of the Creative Arts Center of Chatham where her works have earned awards in members' exhibits. Her inspiration comes from New England's landscape, changing seasons and fantastic light.

TABLE OF CONTENTS

CHARMS OF CHATHAM — *Appetizers & Beverages* ...PAGE 7

Photograph by Betsy Bray ~ Betsy began to pursue her interest in photography in retirement. An intrepid traveler, she has studied with Dr. Fred Kavalier and her work has been exhibited in The Gallery at Cape Cod Photo in Orleans. Capturing the Cape's beautiful light and vistas continues to be her passion.

COMMEMORATIVES — *Soups, Salads & More* ...PAGE 27

Watercolor by Barbara Goldrick ~ Barbara began studying watercolor in Washington D.C. Since her move to Cape Cod she has continued her art studies with Cape Cod artists, Charles Decarlo, Wendy Olin and Robert Mesrop. Barbara finds watercolor to be the ideal medium utilizing transparency and luminous glazes.

COASTAL — *Seafood* ...PAGE 51

Photograph by Margo Karbel ~ Margot has enjoyed taking photographs of people and places since childhood. She does it for fun and to record memories and loves sharing with friends and family. The picture of fishing boats in Aunt Lydia's Cove was taken from the fish pier deck on a beautiful, clear August afternoon in 2010.

COMMUNITY — *Meats & Poultry* ...PAGE 77

Photograph by Eunice Geist ~ Eunice developed her interest in photography as a travel agent and during many trips offering beautiful photo opportunities. She is an active member of the Women's Club and keeps a photographic record of Chatham Garden Club activities.

COMPETITIONS — *Casseroles & Vegetables* ...PAGE 105

Painting by Judith Kelley ~ Judith focused on decorative painting for 15 years. More recently, through courses at the Creative Arts Center, she has enjoyed painting landscapes in acrylic. Her favorite subjects are shells, fish and other sea creatures and scenes of Chatham.

CELEBRATIONS — *Desserts* ...PAGE 125

Hooked rug by Gail Tilton ~ Gail retired to Chatham from elementary school teaching and operating her gift store where she taught decorative painting. She created and sold unique pieces of hand crafted folk art. Rug hooking became painting with wool. In 2009 she designed and completed her first hooked rug in celebration of her daughter's wedding.

SKETCHES *by Madonna Hitchcock, Gail Tilton & Sue Simpson*

Gail Tilton ~ See above. Madonna Hitchcock, a recovering Art History major, has been a cocktail napkin artist for many years. She has studied in taverns, cafés and restaurants throughout the United States and Europe. She received her art education degree from the University of Maryland. Sue Simpson, a computer science major, admits to enjoying sketching for this book.

God bless our fishermen.
May the waters be calm and the nets be full!!

CHARMS OF CHATHAM

Photograph by Betsy Bray

Appetizers & Beverages

The Loop

There is nothing that celebrates the flavor of Chatham more than a walk around the loop! The 3-mile walk begins at Oyster Pond Beach where you savor the scenic water views of swimming floats and boats at anchor as you set off down Stage Harbor Road. The gardens of the lovely homes, large and small, provide a palette of seasonal colors. A left turn onto Bridge Street takes you to the Mitchell River Bridge which divides the beauty of Stage Harbor from the tranquility of Mill Pond. Up ahead you see the sweep of Chatham Light and across the street the ever-popular overlook where the rhythm of the tides serves up a changing menu of beach and ocean. Resuming the walk you pass through the Old Village and continue down Main Street. Turn left at the corner to stroll past the blocks of small stores that supply the spice and zest of life to residents and visitors alike. Striding past the Orpheum Theater and turning left again toward Oyster Pond, you find yourself making a full circle from the starting point. This essence of Chatham is yours to discover every day!

~Barbara Sifflard

BAKED STUFFED QUAHOGS

Ingredients:
   12-15 large quahogs
   2 sleeves Ritz Crackers
   ½ cup panko bread crumbs
   1 garlic clove, minced
   2 tablespoons minced onion
   2 tablespoons butter: plus 1 tablespoon
   ½ cup chopped linguiça
   1 teaspoon hot sauce
   Paprika
   Juice of quahog for desired consistency

Steps:
- Open quahogs, reserve some juice. Chop
- Clean 15 shell halves and wipe the inside of the shells with 1 tablespoon butter; set on a cookie sheet
- Sauté 2 tablespoons butter with garlic and onion until translucent
- Add two sleeves of crushed crackers and panko, quahogs, linguiça and hot sauce
- Mix together adding juice to desired stuffing consistency
- Mound filling in shell and sprinkle with paprika
- Bake 25 minutes at 350°

This is my husband's favorite. Both he and my father are always competing to see who can make the best stuffed quahogs. They go scratching and bring home the fresh catch and make them up. Great served with Chowdah and crusty bread.

~Robin Zibrat

By the Sea

Chatham is a quaint, cozy town
Nestled with water all around,
Houses and gardens shout to say
Our owners give us love each day.
Beaches and parks where children play
Hotels and inns where people stay,
Hang up your hat, put your feet in sand,
Join any group, they are all grand.
Come to Chatham and you will see
Everyone is as helpful as can be,
The kindest people who live by the sea.

~Ann Pronovost Buckley

Summer Tourists

Chatham is a tourist town. Our normally quiet lives change radically for a few months every year. Come the summer we host hordes of people, often with pets, boats and bicycles, who in search of summer fun, arrive by car, bus, motorcycle, van or mobile home. We are honored they have chosen Chatham but things get complicated. Tourists exhibit their enthusiasm by taking pictures, often in the middle of the street. We see them pouring out of tour buses, slowing down for every water view, ignoring pedestrian walkways (we do that too, but we live here), all the while talking on some sort of electronic device. We appreciate their fondness for our town, its shops and its restaurants, but it would be nice not to have to worry about tourist safety. Admittedly, we don't always make it easy for them. The lack of parking is stressful enough, but how to explain Route 28 signs that direct cars to drive "south" to Orleans? Tourists. Love 'em or not, just keep in mind that at some time all of us will be tourists ourselves - confused, enthusiastic and probably annoying.

~Carol Pacun

MOM'S CLAM DIP

Ingredients:
- 1 (8 ounce) package cream cheese
- 1 (8 ounce) can of minced clams
- 1 tablespoon clam juice (from can)
- 1 tablespoon fresh sweet white onion, finely chopped or minced
- ½ teaspoon mayonnaise
- ½ teaspoon lemon juice
- ¼ teaspoon prepared horseradish

Steps:
- Put all ingredients into a bowl
- Mix well with a fork
- Refrigerate

Note: Proportions of onion, mayo, lemon juice and horseradish can be adjusted to taste.

This is a clam dip recipe I inherited from my mother. She served it at picnics at our Cape summer cottage and it became a staple on Sundays for our family during the football season. This is easy to make; it takes less than 10 minutes. Although best served with Ruffle Chips or raw veggies, I love it on a warm piece of toast for lunch.

~Eve Dalmolen

SMOKED OYSTER PÂTÉ

Ingredients:
    2 cans smoked oysters, mashed
    1 bunch scallions
    Small bunch parsley or cilantro
    Worcestershire sauce
    1½ tablespoons mayonnaise
    1½ (8 ounce) packages cream cheese
       (Neufchâtel is fine.)

Steps:
- Mix together all but the cheese
- Roll out the cream cheese between two sheets of plastic wrap into a rectangle about ¼" thick
- Put oyster mixture down the center of the cheese, leaving enough cheese to wrap around the entire oyster mixture
- Wrap the cheese on all sides, pinch to seal edges
- Turn it over so the seams are on the bottom
- Garnish with parsley or cilantro
- Serve with crackers

I have made this for parties for years. It's always a hit with people who enjoy smoked seafood!
~Karen Schwalm

Chatham Smartphone Tour
eTourChatham.org

We have traveled to many cities that have tourist apps for smartphones. My husband decided that Chatham has enough attractions to benefit from a smartphone tour of its own. As part of Chatham's tercentennial celebrations, he designed, wrote and organized the eTour and gave it to Chatham as a gift. The eTour is web-based, free and can be viewed on a home computer as well as on a smartphone or tablet as you wander around town. It is now part of "Historic Chatham", a collaboration of the town's museums and historic sites that continues to focus on Chatham's rich history. The eTour was placed in the tercentennial time capsule.

As he researched sites and descriptions, our entire extended family learned much about Chatham's history. With over 50 locations, the Chatham eTour includes all the historic points of interest as well as hidden gems around town. You can use it while walking or biking through Chatham, or just read or listen to it at home on your tablet. It is a wonderful way to learn about our town's fascinating history.

~Deborah Clark

Appetizers & Beverages   11

Houseguest Rules

Twenty-two years ago my family bought a house in Chatham. I had no idea I would fall in love with Cape Cod - especially Chatham. With each visit I learned something about the town. When friends came to visit, I wanted to show them what I had learned and loved about this town for 20 years - in five days! I insisted that they stay long enough to see why I loved Chatham so much. The house rules were simple.

The first rule was they were not to bring a hostess gift but were instructed to enjoy shopping in the village for a lovely memento to remember their visit here. The second rule was that we would create a house kitty for the funds for grocery trips - filling the larder would be a simple matter for anyone going to the market. Everyone made a contribution to the kitty and put it in a pouch on the counter along with a list of wants and needs. When someone decided to go to the grocery store, they took the kitty and grocery shopped. If the kitty got low, we would all feed the kitty. One day I decided to go to the fish market to pick up lobsters so I grabbed the pouch (a sandwich baggie) and stood in line to pay for my fish. A nice man looked at my baggie with curiosity and commented that I had an interesting way of carrying my money. I explained it was the house kitty and it was how we made our house guests more comfortable as they all participated in funding for the house food. He thought that was a brilliant idea and said he was going home to set up a house kitty plan for his steady stream of summer guests.

The third and final rule was about my guests exploring the Cape. I suggested they go out and come back with a discovery that would teach me something I didn't know. That was a challenge for many of my friends; however, I learned many things that I shared with the next group of houseguests.

I now live in Chatham year round and I love it beyond being a tourist. I love the dramatic changes in the weather and getting to know the interesting people who make up this lovely place. It is a delightful village with two independent bookstores and a world class library. My friends love to come visit year after year and many do their Christmas shopping here. They all look forward to the wonderful shellfish and fresh air and the uncluttered landscape of the National Seashore. I am glad to live in a place where my friends love to visit me.

~Lane Byrd

CHEESE STRAWS

Ingredients:
- 1 stick unsalted butter, room temperature
- 1 pound grated extra sharp cheddar cheese, at room temperature
- ½ teaspoon fresh cayenne pepper or to taste
- Salt to taste
- 2 cups self-rising flour
  (If using all-purpose flour, add ¼ teaspoon salt and 2 teaspoon baking powder.)

Steps:
- In a large mixing bowl, mix butter, cheese, red pepper and salt
- Beat until smooth and creamy in food processor
- Add the flour and beat well
- Do not over work the dough
- Let dough rest about 15 minutes
- Run through a cookie press with the star disk
- Bake for 350° for 15 minutes, until almost crisp

Cheese straws are a southern tradition and are always on hand for luncheons, tea parties, weddings and more.

~Lane Byrd

Appetizers & Beverages

Creative Arts Center

The Creative Arts Center (CAC), located on Crowell Road, is dedicated to the teaching and appreciation of the arts. Who knew that this organization would have such a profound effect on my life as a happy retiree and an emerging watercolor artist? My walls attest to the discoveries at the Center's semi-annual "Sacrifice Art Sale," a wonderful introduction to local talent held in July and October.

Now, as a CAC member, I appreciate the Center's scheduled classes, workshops, demonstrations and special programs. Classes in drawing, painting, pottery and jewelry are held regularly and workshops with nationally known artists are held every summer. Exhibitions are mounted in the Center's galleries where students, members, faculty, artists and photographers from Chatham and the Cape region have the opportunity to share their work. On the third weekend in August, CAC sponsors "Festival of the Arts," a juried arts and crafts festival under tents in Chase Park.

~Barbara Gibson

EGGPLANT SPREAD

Ingredients:
- 2 medium eggplants, peeled, cut into 1" cubes
- 1 red bell pepper, seeded, cut into 1" cubes
- 1 Vidalia onion, cut into 1" cubes
- 2 garlic cloves, minced
- 3 tablespoons olive oil
- 1½ teaspoons salt
- ½ teaspoon black ground pepper
- 2 tablespoons lemon juice
- 2 tablespoons tahini sauce
- 2 drops hot sauce (optional)
- 3 tablespoons chopped parsley, plus more for garnish

Steps:
- In large bowl, toss eggplant, bell pepper and onion with olive oil, salt, pepper and garlic.
- Spread on baking sheet, roast 45 minutes at 400° until slightly brown and soft, toss during cooking
- Add roasted vegetables to blender and add in remaining ingredients. Pulse leaving some chunks.
- Garnish with fresh parsley
- Serve with crackers or bread

~Peggy Sullivan Crespo

HERB CHEESE STUFFED MUSHROOMS

Ingredients:
- 2 (8 ounce) packages cream cheese, softened
- 1 (1 ounce) package Hidden Valley Original Ranch salad dressing & seasoning mix
- ½ cup mayonnaise
- 2 tablespoons minced onion or scallions
- 1 tablespoon chopped parsley
- ¼ cup Parmesan cheese, grated
- 3 to 4 strips well cooked bacon, crumbled
- 1½ pounds mushrooms, cleaned with stems removed
- 1 cup crushed Pepperidge Farms herb stuffing mix (grind fine in blender or food processor) or use bread crumbs
- 8 tablespoon melted butter

Steps:
- Preheat oven to 350°
- Mix cream cheese, Ranch mix, mayonnaise, onion, parsley, Parmesan and bacon in food processor
- Stuff mushrooms with cheese mixture
- Dip the top of the filled mushrooms into the crushed stuffing mix
- Place mushrooms on a baking sheet
- Pour melted butter over the top of mushrooms
- Bake for 30 minutes

~Peggy Sullivan Crespo

Galleries

Did you know that Chatham, home of the cod, the clam, the seal and the great white shark also has 17 art galleries? Most galleries are located on Main Street between the rotary and the Chatham Light. The Chatham Gallery Association sponsors Gallery Nights from July through December. Artists represented come from Chatham, Cape Cod, New England and beyond.

Galleries in town showcase fine art, art photography, jewelry, furniture, pottery, framing, appraisals, restoration and art classes. Gallery Association members, the Chatham Guild of Artists and other outlets prove Chatham to be a vibrant, exciting and adventuresome arts destination.

~Barbara Gibson

Italian Appetizer Bites

Ingredients:
- 2 packages refrigerated crescent rolls
- ½ pound deli salami
- ½ pound sliced provolone cheese
- ½ pound sliced deli ham or prosciutto
- 7 eggs
- 1 cup grated Parmesan cheese
- 2 (12 ounce) jars roasted peppers, drained

Steps:
- Heat oven to 350°; coat a 13" x 9" glass baking dish with non-stick cooking spray
- Unroll 1 package of crescent rolls and use dough to line the bottom of dish pinching seams together
- Cover rolls with half of the salami, provolone and ham
- Beat 6 of the eggs with the Parmesan
- Pour half of the egg mixture over the top
- Top with half of the roasted pepper
- Add remaining salami, provolone and ham.
- Pour remaining egg mixture over the top and top with remaining roasted pepper
- Top with the remaining crescent rolls
- Beat remaining egg and brush over top
- Cover dish with foil and bake for 30 minutes
- Uncover and bake for about 30 minutes additional
- Cool for 1 hour and then cut into squares

A great recipe for sharing at a BYOB. Fast, easy, hardy & delicious!

~Karen Schwalm

Cape Abilities Farm to Table Market & Gallery

The shop is easy to find located shortly after Main Street turns in the direction of Chatham Lighthouse. The bright lime color sets it off from the typical Cape Cod grey shingles, as does the Greek Revival architecture. Like much of Chatham, the building has had many transitions. While the color was a surprise to most, it now is a welcome sight to those looking to buy fresh local vegetables and fruit. Much of the produce is from Cape Abilities Farm in Dennis. Works by Cape Cod artists are featured in the Gallery. Furniture pieces are also offered for sale. These are provided by Cape Abilities Furniture Rescue and Restore, a project that gives new life to old furniture and provides jobs for Cape Abilities participants. Many of the staff of the shop are Cape Abilities participants and students from local schools' special needs programs.

The shop was launched in 2011 when the owner of the historic building offered Cape Abilities the use of the space free of rent. Chatham has a history of strong support for this organization that provides a wide variety of services for people with disabilities across the Cape.

~Joanne Donoghue

Chatham's Town Flower Gardens

In the spring of 1968, The Women's Club of Chatham gave birth to the Chatham Garden Club. They were then, and still are, a dedicated group of women gardeners who gather to plant and take care of many of the wonderful public gardens and window boxes that grace our beautiful town. These gardens which help make our town shine on Main Street include the Town Hall window boxes, the horse trough by the Methodist Church and the Sears Park Memorial Garden. The Garden Club also maintains gardens at the Fire Station, the Lighthouse, the Atwood House Museum, the environmental garden at Oyster Pond and the wonderful garden at the Training Field Road triangle. The gardens are one of the many things people look forward to when coming to the Cape.

~Gail Smith

Appetizers & Beverages

Pita Chips

Ingredients:
- 2 pita bread rounds
- Olive oil
- Sea salt
- Freshly ground pepper
- Shredded Parmesan cheese
- Fresh basil

Steps:
- Separate the pita breads top and bottom. Both very thin and thicker bread works.
- Tear into medium irregular pieces and place on a cookie sheet on parchment paper or foil
- Brush each piece with olive oil and salt and pepper liberally
- Sprinkle on shredded cheese
- Scissor cut fresh basil leaves in thin shreds and add on top
- Place in 400° degree oven for up to five minutes, watching carefully for edges to brown slightly and cheese and oil to bubble. Or broil for a minute or two.
- Serve on a colorful platter.

Note: Melted butter or mayonnaise can be used to coat the bread pieces. If more uniform wedges suit you, use a knife to cut bread into that shape. For a spicy southwestern taste, ground red pepper flakes, shredded Monterey Jack and cilantro, in addition to salt and pepper, can be used. For a simple but delicious flavor, use mayonnaise, salt and pepper only.

~Regina McDowell

Movies Return to Main Street

If you are looking to enjoy a first run or classic film, a thought provoking documentary, or an inspiring foreign film, then the Chatham Orpheum Theater is just the place for you! Originally opened in 1916, the Orpheum operated year round offering a variety of films. Many are delighted to return to a modern version of their favorite childhood theater where they enjoyed viewing movies with parents and grandparents.

ARTICHOKE TARTS

Ingredients:
- Cooking spray
- 16 pieces wonton wrappers
- ¼ cup low-fat shredded cheddar cheese
- 4 ounces softened fat free cream cheese
- ¼ teaspoon cayenne pepper
- 1 (7 ounce) can drained & chopped artichoke hearts
- ¼ cup fresh parsley sprigs
- ½ tablespoon Dijon mustard
- 2 tablespoons chopped sweet red pepper

Steps:
- Preheat oven to 350°
- Coat a mini muffin pan with cooking spray
- Gently press 1 wonton wrapper into each muffin hole, allowing ends to extend above cups
- Coat edges of wrappers with cooking spray
- In medium bowl, mix cheese, cayenne pepper and mustard
- Stir in red pepper and artichoke hearts
- Spoon about 1 teaspoon of cheese mixture into each muffin cup
- Bake about 12-15 minutes. Garnish with parsley.

One of my family's favorite recipes.
~Fran Monroe

As a weekly volunteer, I enjoy meeting the patrons and experiencing their enthusiastic response. As they enter the lobby, they comment on the nostalgic aroma of the freshly popped popcorn. Many are captivated by the hand painted mural which depicts numerous movie stars dressed in the attire of a defining role as well as their famous directors. Others are delighted to be able to purchase a savory snack or a glass of wine to be enjoyed in a comfortable seat in one of the two theaters. Hope to see you at the Chatham Orpheum Theater soon!

~Claire Balfour

Appetizers & Beverages

CANDIED WALNUT CRANBERRY SPREAD

Ingredients:
- ⅓ cup walnut pieces, chopped medium
- 1 tablespoon brown sugar
- 1 teaspoon vanilla extract
- 1 tablespoon honey
- 1 (8 ounce) package cream cheese, softened
- ⅓ cup honey
- ⅓ cup dried cranberries

Step:
- Toss first 4 ingredients to combine
- Bake at 350° for 10 minutes
- Combine the next 3 ingredients and the candied walnut pieces and mix well
- Store in refrigerator and about ½ hour before serving remove to make it spreadable
- Serve with crackers
- Yield: 2 cups

I serve this at holiday time but it gets great reviews any time of the year!
~Susan Adsit

Cranberries

Fall is a beautiful time in Chatham. While most of New England boasts spectacular fall foliage, we have the added beauty of gorgeous blankets of red berries, ready for harvest, on the cranberry bogs of Cape Cod. Cranberries, along with blueberries and Concord grapes, are the only fruits that are native to North America. Today cranberry bogs make up about 40 percent of agriculture on Cape Cod. Chatham currently has four active cranberry bogs. In the past, other wetland areas were converted to cranberry production, but over time these were filled and developed, prior to wetland regulations or were let go and have since returned to natural wetlands. Cranberries add a touch of Cape Cod to baked goods, pancakes, muffins, salads and other recipes.

~Laurie LaConte

Cranberry Glazed Brie

Ingredients:
  1 Brie – 8 inch in diameter, about 2.2 pounds
Topping:
  3 cups cranberries
  ¾ cup brown sugar
  ⅓ cup water
  ⅛ teaspoon dry mustard
  ⅛ teaspoon allspice
  ⅛ teaspoon cardamom
  ⅛ teaspoon ground cloves
  ⅛ teaspoon ginger

Steps:
- Combine and cook the topping ingredients over medium heat until the berries pop
- The mixture should be thick after cooking
- Remove from the stove and cool
- Cut and remove a circle of the Brie rind - discard
- Add topping and heat at 350° for 12 minutes
- Serve with sliced pears and apples or crackers

This is a wonderful appetizer at Christmas or whenever. The topping can be prepared up to 3 days before serving.
~Rita Broman

Fig & Brie Torte

Ingredients:
  1 (8 ounce) wheel of Brie
  1 (8 ounce) jar fig spread
  ½ cup chopped macadamia nuts (or walnuts)
  Crackers or bagel rounds

Steps:
- Place Brie in refrigerator for about 2 hours to firm up for easier slicing
- Preheat oven to 350°
- Using a sharp knife or dental floss, slice Brie in half horizontally into two rounds
- Distribute the fig spread evenly atop the bottom layer of the round, avoiding the ¼ inch closest to the edge so that the jam doesn't spill over when the top layer is sandwiched on
- Sprinkle chopped macadamia nuts over the fig spread
- Add the top layer of the Brie wheel.
- Bake at 350° for about 15 minutes until cheese is melted
- Transfer to a serving dish and surround with crackers or bagel rounds

~Joanne Lowre

Friends of Trees

In the 1960s and 1970s the fine old elm trees that graced Main Street and other streets in Chatham began to succumb to Dutch elm disease. In response to this tragic development, Friends of Trees (FOT) was founded in 1975. With the help of contributions from the town's concerned citizens, trees began to be replanted. Friends of Trees became a non-profit organization in 1983. Its efforts have been supported by donations from individuals and businesses, grants and from requests for the planting of memorial trees. Since its founding, Friends of Trees has planted and cared for over 2,000 trees and shrubs that survive and thrive in this demanding seaside climate.

In an effort to foster good stewardship and to enhance the community's understanding and appreciation for the value of trees, FOT initiated educational programs for children, walking tours to view notable trees, and in 2013, sponsored Arbor Day in recognition of the value of trees to Chatham's community.

~Lee Kimball

The Swinging Basket

Chatham Gardens on Main Street, formerly The Swinging Basket, may have been the very first gift shop on the Cape. It was established in the early 1920s. Many of the early plantings are still thriving. Some of the rare specimens that remain are the Japanese Umbrella Plant, Australian Cedars and River Birch in the courtyard, as well as a Japanese Maple covering the once active wishing well in the back. The building in the rear was the Western Union Building brought to this location years ago. At the back entrance, a little tollgate allowed entry by pitching in a few coins. The antique black town clock in front on Main Street was erected in 2008. What a small, hidden gem of Chatham!!

~Fleur Jones

PEAR & ALMOND CROUSTADE

Ingredients:
- Pastry for one crust pie
- 4 ripe but firm Bartlett pears peeled, cored and sliced
- ¼ cup apricot preserves
- 2 tablespoons brown sugar
- ¾ teaspoon almond extract
- ½ teaspoon cinnamon

Topping:
- 2 tablespoons flour
- 1½ tablespoons butter
- 1 tablespoon brown sugar
- 2 tablespoons sliced almonds

Steps:
- Preheat oven to 400°
- Lay pastry on large parchment lined baking sheet
- Mix pears with all ingredients except those for topping
- Pile pear filling in the center of the pastry and bring about 2 inch edge up around the filling, folding as you go
- Mix the topping ingredients except the almonds to form crumbs and sprinkle on top of the pear filling
- Top with almonds
- Bake 20-25 minutes until golden brown
- Let cool at least 30 minutes before serving

~Judi Clifford

Dad's Punch

Ingredients:
- 1 liter Seagram's VO
- 1 liter ginger ale
- 1 liter club soda
- 1 liter Tom Collins mix
- 1 (12 ounce) can frozen pink lemonade, thawed
- 1 ice block

Ice Block Ingredients:
- 1 jar of maraschino cherries
- Pineapple rings depending on number of batches

Steps:
- Chill all liters
- Just prior to serving, mix all together in punch bowl
- Add ice block

Ice Block Steps:
- Use a container the size of a medium cool whip container
- Fill half with water and place in freezer until slushy
- Remove from freezer and add pineapple ring to center; surround with cherries
- Return to freezer until frozen
- Fill the rest of the container with water and freeze
- To remove ice block from container, place in hot water for a short time to loosen

Every year my parents had a large open house at Christmas and my Dad made this punch. He made it in a large punch bowl and served it in punch cups. It was delicious but packed a "punch."

~Ann Wade

Appetizers & Beverages

CAPE COD MARGARITA

Ingredients:
- 1½ ounce tequila
- 1 ounce sweet lime juice
- 1 ounce triple sec
- 2 ounces cranberry juice (pure juice, not cocktail)
- 1½ ounce sour mix (50/50 mix of frozen concentrated lemonade & limeade)

Steps:
- Mix equal portions of frozen concentrated lemonade and limeade to make sour mix
- Using proportions above make the number of drinks desired
- Mix ingredients and keep chilled
- Serve over ice in margarita glasses with or without salt

My son was married in Chatham and we spent a few weeks before the wedding tasting to find the perfect signature drink for the rehearsal party. Everyone loved our Cape Cod drink.
~Deborah Clark

Mooncussers

When I came to Chatham, I kept hearing the word "Mooncussers." I had no idea what it meant so I did some local research. Legends say that in the 18th and 19th century up and down our coastline some "not so upstanding people" lured boats to go aground on the tricky shores. They would place lanterns in areas that were dangerous and when ships neared, they would wave the lanterns drawing them in. In those days there were not many lighthouses and their power was not strong. The sailors would see the lanterns and come closer to shore. Once the ships wrecked, the villains would salvage the cargo. But if there was a moon, even a half moon, the sailors could see and not be fooled. The villains would "Cuss the Moon" and over time they became known as the "Mooncussers." However, some historians believe that there were no "Mooncussers" on our shores but that there were many so called "wreckers." They would help save the sailors from the wrecked ships and then take the cargo. Accordingly, many Chatham homes were well stocked with many salvaged items. The debate goes on!

~Ann Wade

Mural Barn

One of the many treasures of the Atwood House Museum is the Alice Stallknecht paintings displayed in the Mural Barn. Few people come to visit the museum exclusively to view these murals but when they take the time to see them they are usually delighted and charmed by their history.

As a volunteer in the Mural Barn on Friday mornings during the summer I have the enviable task of talking about the murals to visitors from all over the United States and from foreign countries. What is most interesting are visitors who recall the people and the events depicted in these paintings:

- The elderly gentleman who remembered working at the Hawes Boarding House as a teenager. "People did not stay more than a week because the same menu was repeated week after week."
- The Harwich man who knew most of the fishermen in the "Every Man to His Trade" panels.
- The Mural Barn volunteer who was painted as a small child in the panels entitled "Christ Preaching to the Multitudes."

What a wonderful gift Alice Stallknecht gave to the Town!

~Florence Seldin

Commemoratives

Stage Harbor Light — Painting by Barbara Goldrick

Soups, Salads & More

The Old Village

The Old Village neighborhood surrounding Chatham Light is one of the town's oldest. In earlier times, the "village" was the center of the town, with shops and businesses serving the bustling maritime activities just below the twin lighthouses. Tides, storms and breakthroughs changed all that. The business district and the fish pier moved elsewhere. Beach-front buildings were moved to higher ground and most old shops were turned into homes as summer residents joined locals to form a tightly knit community which preferred to think of the area, not as a cluster of houses, but as a state of mind.

Living jam-packed together in a place where everyone walks—and talks—a good deal, we have bonded to keep our neighborhood history alive and to stress the importance of protecting it. This has not been an easy task. At the edge of an unpredictable often violent ocean, we have seen houses fall into the water, our beach destroyed and our once quiet shoreline become one of the Cape's most popular destinations. But, working together, we have largely prevailed: forming a local association, helping the town save Andrew Hardings Lane beach for public use, protesting violently against unseemly state projects and forming a National Historic District. The challenges continue unabated, but I trust that our underlying belief that past, present and future must be linked together will help us preserve what we love.

~Carol Pacun

SUMMER TOMATO LEMON SOUP

Ingredients:
- 3 cups tomato juice
- 2 tablespoons tomato paste
- 4 scallions, minced
- Salt to taste
- Pinch of powdered thyme
- ½ teaspoon curry powder
- Freshly ground pepper
- Grated rind of ½ lemon
- 2 tablespoons fresh lemon juice
- 1 teaspoon sugar
- 1 cup sour cream
- Chopped parsley, if desired

Steps:
- Mix all the ingredients except the sour cream and parsley
- Blend in sour cream
- Chill thoroughly for at least 2 hours
- Sprinkle with chopped parsley, if desired and serve

Serves 4-6

A cool summer delight!
~Pat Vreeland

Chatham's Life Saving Stations

In 1872, Congress authorized life saving stations for the Outer Cape and four of them were built in Chatham. Life Saving Station Number 13 was built in 1872 near the present day Monomoy Wildlife Refuge headquarters on Morris Island. Monomoy Station was built a year later and was located just north of the Monomoy Light. In 1897, Old Harbor Station was constructed on North Beach across from Minister's Point and five years later, the fourth station, Monomoy Point Station was established on the southern tip of Monomoy. In 1977, the Old Harbor Station was moved to Provincetown to become a museum at the Cape Cod National Seashore.

By 1955, all search and rescue operations were consolidated into the U.S. Coast Guide operations at the Chatham Lighthouse. Today the mission of helping those "in peril upon the seas" remains, now performed by the Chatham Coast Guard.

~Sharon Oudemool

CHILLED CUCUMBER SOUP

Ingredients:
- 3 cucumbers, peeled, seeded and grated
- 3 cucumbers, peeled, seeded and chopped
- 2 cloves garlic
- ½ cup packed parsley leaves
- ½ cup lemon juice
- ½ cup sour cream
- 1½ quarts buttermilk
- 1 tablespoon kosher salt
- 1 teaspoon white lemon pepper
- 2 cups water

Garnish:
- 1 chopped cucumber
- Scallions as needed
- Mint as needed

Steps:
- In a food processor purée the 3 chopped cucumbers with the garlic, parsley, lemon juice and sour cream
- Combine the 3 grated cucumbers with the rest of the ingredients
- Adjust seasoning to taste
- Garnish with chopped cucumber, scallions and mint

This is a delicious soup. A fun presentation at a party is to ladle it into small votive holders.
   ~Madonna Hitchcock

Chatham in War

Because of Chatham's strategic geographical location, this area has had an important role in several wars. In the Revolutionary War, the British fleet blockaded the coast. This closed the harbor and caused fishing boats to fall into disrepair. Many men were out of work. The British launched a foray by privateers into the harbor but they were repelled by the local militia led by Captain Godfrey and were sent back into the Atlantic.

VICHYSSOISE

Ingredients:
- 1 large potato (Idaho) cut in ½ inch slices
- 1 leek (white part only) cut in 1½ inch slices
- 1 can chicken broth with 1 can water
- ½ cup cream (or non-fat half and half)
- Chopped chives

Steps:
- Cook potato, leek and broth in covered microwave dish for 10 minutes. Test with a fork so that the potato and leek are soft but not mushy
- Cool uncovered for about one minute
- Put in blender. Remove center of blender cover to allow steam to escape
- Blend until all mixed and creamy
- Put in bowl and refrigerate (can make in the morning or even day before)
- When ready to serve, whisk in the cream
- Serve with chives on top of each serving

Serves 4-6

This a very easy and yummy soup and is great for Chatham summers.

~Prudence Davies

In the War of 1812 most local men enlisted in the military, the majority as navigators in the Navy on ships patrolling the coast.

In the Civil War 292 men enlisted, a huge majority of the local men. Many died in battles in Cold Harbor, Spotsylvania, Petersburg and in the prison camp at Andersonville. Only a few returned to Chatham after the war.

~Mary Ann Chamberlain

The Year the Blimp Came to Town

It was the summer of 1966 when the Goodyear Blimp came to Chatham Airport. A reporter from the Boston Record American envisioned a dynamite publicity stunt: the Blimp would pull a water skier. How to make it happen? First, go to the Mitchell River Marina, now Stage Harbor Marine. Next, rent equipment and a boat with a captain to carry the equipment. And finally, inquire if anyone knew someone who might be able to waterski in back of the Blimp. It was suggested that one of the lifeguards at the Oyster Pond might just be interested and able. She was and a plan was hatched. Alas, though she was willing, able and up on her skis, the Oyster Pond was not big enough for the Blimp to maneuver and she had nowhere to ski. Where to go? Pleasant Bay! If one skier was good, two would be great! Her younger brother was game. Pleasant Bay was perfect and the two had a great time waterskiing as well as a wonderful tale to tell.

~Ann Hosmer

The Mitchell River Bridge

In 2002-03, the Chatham Women's Club decided to raise much needed funds by selling sweatshirts with a Chatham drawing by Ursula Romero on the front. For that drawing, she chose the Mitchell River Bridge as a symbol of Chatham's history. This sentiment proved to be accurate as two decades later the bridge was honored as the last single leaf wooden drawbridge in the country. Time passes. Now, ironically, in the club's 100 anniversary year, the Mitchell River Bridge is to be replaced by a more modern structure. Yet, memories of the bridge as it was drawn on club sweatshirts will linger on, especially for those of us who drove over the bridge regularly, threw fishing lines over its sides or crossed it on foot. Most special were

Gazpacho

Ingredients:
- 10 large ripe tomatoes, peeled, seeded and cut into chunks
- 15 ounces chicken consommé or broth
- 1 cucumber, peeled and sliced
- 1 medium green pepper, chopped
- ½ large white onion, diced
- 1 bunch salad onions, chopped; reserve ⅔ green tops for garnish
- 3 cloves of garlic
- Condiments: Salt, sugar, a little pepper, olive oil, red wine vinegar, freshly squeezed lemon juice*
- Herbs: lots of fresh basil, tarragon, chervil and fresh mint*
- Sour cream for garnish (optional garnishes: watercress, sliced radishes and lemons)

Steps:
- Crush the garlic and thoroughly rub bottom and sides of a 2½ quart bowl
- Add all * ingredients to your taste, as when dressing a salad
- Add tomatoes and any juice from them, consommé, cucumbers, peppers and onions
- Adjust seasoning before chilling
- Cover and refrigerate overnight, or for at least four hours
- When serving: add a dollop of sour cream topped with the chopped green onions
- Add other garnishes of your choice

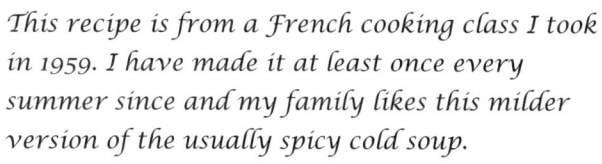

This recipe is from a French cooking class I took in 1959. I have made it at least once every summer since and my family likes this milder version of the usually spicy cold soup.

~Barbara Schweizer

---

the times when the bridge was raised for boats to pass through. We all stopped, often leaving our cars to enjoy the beauty of the scene or watch the ancient wooden deck lumber upward and then settle back down. In this memorable year, I think how both the Women's Club and the bridge, such different entities, have played a part in bringing us closer to our very special town. Whatever changes time brings, this is a gift that will remain with us.

~Carol Pacun

Soups, Salads & More

Captain George N. Harding Conservation Area

Captain George N. Harding was my grandfather and a property on Route 28 in West Chatham is named in his honor. The land was purchased in 2004 by the Town of Chatham using Land Bank funds and will be preserved as open space.

Born on March 8, 1865, George N. Harding spent most of his life at sea. In his early teens, George went with his father aboard the four-masted schooner, the Henry L. Peckham. Shortly after joining the Boston Marine Society he became captain and part owner of the schooner. He made regular cargo runs, often accompanied by his wife, to ports along the Eastern seaboard.

In 1915, Captain Harding joined the U.S. Lightship Service--the precursor of the U.S. Coast Guard--as Master of Lightship 85, famously known as the Nantucket. This lightship was stationed approximately 40 miles SW of Nantucket Island. This ship served as an important beacon to passing vessels using the busy shipping lanes near the very dangerous Nantucket Shoals. Captain Harding retired from the Lightship Service in 1935. He spent his remaining days in his family home located on this site until his death in 1935.

~Linda Hennigan

CLAM BISQUE

Ingredients:
- ⅓ cup butter
- ⅓ cup flour
- Juice of 2 cans of minced clams. Set aside the clams
- 2 cups half and half
- 1 can (8 ounce) of tomato sauce
- 1 can (14.5 ounce) diced tomatoes
- 1 bay leaf
- 1 teaspoon ground thyme
- 1 teaspoon curry

Steps:
- In a medium sauce pan, make a roux with the butter and flour
- Add remaining ingredients except the clams
- Stir until smooth and bring to a simmer
- Simmer for 30 minutes, stirring occasionally
- Just before serving add the clams and heat until hot

Note: Easily doubled to use as a main course with a salad and Artisan bread

Serves 6

A quick and easy recipe to precede the main course. Can be done ahead and warmed up before serving.

~Eileen Gibb

Soups, Salads & More

Shanties on Oyster River

Have you ever wondered about the buildings at the end of Barn Hill Landing? For decades, these shanties have stood at the end of the Oyster River just before the bend. The shell fishermen brought in their catch of quahogs, steamer clams, bay and sea scallops, oysters and mussels for selling. Most of the shanties do not have electricity. They are rented to shell fishermen so they can store their equipment, park their vehicles and moor their boats.

Over time, the ownership of the buildings has changed very little and part of the property is still owned by the original family. In the early days, the fishermen shucked their catch and sold it. Now there is no more shucking done at the shanties and the sale of the catch is done through companies that distribute to retailers.

The shanties are part of Chatham's shell fishing history and continue today as a valuable resource for many shell fishermen in our community.

~Ann Wade

SCALLOP SOUP

Ingredients:
- 1½ pounds sea scallops
- 3 tablespoons butter
- 3 tablespoons flour
- 4 cups half and half
- 1 teaspoon chicken flavored bouillon granules
- ⅛ teaspoon white pepper
- 1 package petite peas defrosted
- ½ cup sherry

Steps:
- Wash scallops
- Remove and discard the small vertical band attached to the side of the scallop
- Cut scallops in half and set aside
- Melt butter in a heavy saucepan over low heat
- Add flour, stirring until smooth
- Cook 1 minute stirring constantly
- Gradually add half and half
- Cook over low heat, stirring constantly until thickened and bubbly
- Stir in scallops, bouillon granules, pepper and peas
- Cook over low heat 10 minutes, stirring frequently. Do not allow it to boil
- Stir in sherry

Makes 4 medium servings

A delicious Chatham treat for out-of-town guests.

~Joanne Donoghue

Winter Squash & Shrimp Chowder

Ingredients:
- 3 tablespoons unsalted butter
- 1⅓ cups finely chopped scallions using both green tops and white bulbs
- 1 small red bell pepper, seeded, finely chopped
- ¼ cup chopped fresh parsley
- 2 tablespoons chopped fresh basil or 1 teaspoon dried basil
- 1 (2 pound) butternut squash, peeled, seeded and diced
- 1 small ham bone or ½ pound of smoked ham
- 1 quart chicken broth
- ½ teaspoon ground allspice
- ¼ teaspoon ground mace
- Pinch of ground nutmeg
- 2 medium potatoes (1¼ pounds) peeled, diced
- 1 cup heavy cream at room temperature
- ½ pound fresh shrimp, shelled, deveined and cut into pieces

Steps:
- Melt butter in Dutch oven over medium low heat
- Add scallions, cook 3 minutes
- Stir in bell pepper, cook 3 additional minutes
- Add parsley, basil, squash and ham
- Stir well and add chicken stock
- Sprinkle with allspice, mace and nutmeg
- Heat to boiling
- Reduce heat and simmer partially covered for 25 minutes
- Add potatoes and cream
- Return mixture to boiling; reduce heat
- Simmer, partially covered, until the potatoes are tender (approximately 25 minutes)
- Remove ham bone.
- Add shrimp to chowder.
- Cook, uncovered, over low heat until shrimp turns pink, about 3-4 minutes.

Serves 6

An easy yet flavorful chowder. A family favorite!
~Mary Melo

PORTUGUESE KALE SOUP

Ingredients:
- 1 cup pea beans
- 1 large onion, sliced
- 1 pound chorizo sausage (highly spiced sausage)
- 1 pound kale
- 1 tablespoon salt
- ½ teaspoon pepper
- 1 tablespoon vinegar
- 2 cups cubed potatoes

Steps:
- Soak beans overnight in cold water
- In the morning, drain and add the onion, sausage (cut in pieces), kale (broken into pieces, stem removed), salt, pepper, vinegar and 10 cups water
- Bring to a boil, reduce heat and cook gently 2-3 hours
- Add potatoes and 1 additional cup water
- Continue cooking until potatoes are tender

Serves 6

I have made this recipe many times and it's the best I have eaten. I've been interested in the influence of the Portuguese fishermen, who came to the Cape and left a legacy.

~Marta Dutkewych

Historians

As historians for The Women's Club of Chatham, we sort and file pictures, newspaper articles and records that span the one hundred years of the club's existence. Through these papers, we have learned about a group of women who came together to be a positive force in their community and also formed strong bonds and friendships.

From May baskets and food sales, parties, raffles and garden tours the non-profit organization has raised impressive amounts of money. The funds raised have gone for scholarships, veterans' needs and grants to community organizations. There have been large projects such as establishing the Visiting Nurse Association in Chatham and small projects such as purchasing a bicycle for a handicapped child. It is very clear to us that the club's new motto, Connecting Women--Enriching Community, is as timely for the past as it is for today.

~Nancy Black and Laurie Bonin

The Silver Service

When I was little, I would visit my Grandma Teen. One day she was busy making tea sandwiches of cucumbers and cream cheese. She was going to her meeting of the Chatham Woman's Club. My grandmother was the treasurer of the club for many years and had joined in the 60s. I asked her what she was going to do at her meeting and she said, "I'm going to be the pourer!" I had no idea what this meant. She continued to explain that the women would have tea and coffee and she was in charge of sitting at the silver service and pouring the tea.

Years later I joined the Women's Club and got to see what the pourer did. We had two magnificent silver teapots on shiny silver trays. The table was decorated with flowers and petite sandwiches and cookies were arranged on pretty plates. Lemon slices and cream and sugar sat in polished bowls. I was excited to finally see what a "pourer" did. It was an honor for several of the older ladies to be asked to pour the tea. We used china cups and tea plates. It was beautiful and elegant. When the meeting was over, we lovingly cleaned the service and packed it away in soft cloths for the next meeting.

A generation later we still enjoy our silver tea service for special occasions. In this new world of convenience, however, we substitute it with shiny coffee urns for our monthly meetings.

~Robin Zibrat

Spring~Summer Strawberry Salad

Ingredients:
- 1 head Boston lettuce, washed, dried and torn into pieces
- 6-8 strawberries, sliced
- ¼ cup pecans, toasted*
- 3-4 ounces goat cheese, chilled

Salad Dressing:
- ⅓ cup olive oil
- 2½ tablespoons balsamic vinegar
- ¼ teaspoon (scant) curry powder
- 1½ tablespoons sugar
- Salt and pepper

Steps:
- Make the dressing
- Mix together the lettuce, strawberries and pecans. Toss with enough dressing to cover
- Break goat cheese into small clumps. Sprinkle over salad

* Note: I have also used glazed pecans, untoasted. This gives more sweetness counterpointing the cheese.
Serves 4

A delicious. Lovely salad for warm seasons.
~Karen Schwalm

Watermelon Salad

Ingredients:
- 1 cup Israeli couscous
- 4 pounds watermelon (cut into cubes)
- 2 cups arugula (packed)
- 8 ounces feta cheese
- 2 lemons
- ¼ cup extra virgin olive oil
- 2 tablespoons honey
- 1 teaspoon salt
- ½ teaspoon pepper

Steps:
- Cook Israeli couscous to package directions and cool
- Whisk grated zest and juice of 2 lemons, extra virgin olive oil, honey, salt and pepper
- Set dressing aside
- Combine watermelon, cubed feta, arugula and couscous
- Toss with dressing

Listen to the crowd cheer. It is the most popular salad of the summer.
~Madonna Hitchcock

Mandarin Orange Salad

Salad Ingredients:
- 4 cups lettuce
- 4 cups spinach (or red leaf lettuce)
- 1 cup chopped celery
- ½ cup sliced green onion
- ½ cup slivered almonds
- 3 tablespoons sugar
- 1 (11 ounce) can mandarin oranges

Salad Dressing:
- ⅓ cup oil
- ¼ cup sugar
- ¼ cup white vinegar
- 1 tablespoon chopped parsley
- ½ teaspoon hot pepper

Steps:
- In a skillet, cook the almonds and sugar over medium low heat until sugar melts
- Cool on a tray or nonstick surface
- In large bowl, combine first four ingredients
- Toss with dressing
- Add oranges and almonds

What makes this salad so tasty is the dressing. My family always loves to see it on special occasions.
~Rita Broman

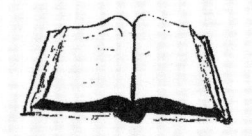

Ladies Reading Club

Book Clubs are very popular on Cape Cod and Chatham is no exception. It is not uncommon to meet women who belong to several book groups. One of the most interesting is the Chatham Ladies Reading Club founded in 1911 and still going strong. Back then women from all over Chatham gathered once a week for information, enrichment and to exchange ideas. These women established The Chatham Historical Society and in 1924 they raised enough funds to buy and renovate the Atwood House Museum.

ORIENTAL BROCCOLI SALAD

Salad Ingredients:
- 1½ packages broccoli slaw
- 1 red pepper, chopped
- 3-4 green onions, chopped
- 1 cup sunflower kernel seeds or pine nuts
- 1 cup sliced/slivered almonds, toasted
- 2 packages Ramen oriental soup mix (crush the noodles and add to the salad uncooked)

Dressing Ingredients:
- 2 flavor packets from the soup mix
- 1 cup olive oil
- ½ cup sugar
- ⅓ cup balsamic vinegar

Steps:
- Mix first 6 ingredients together in a large bowl
- Mix dressing ingredients and pour over broccoli mix
- Serve in a large bowl
- Makes a huge salad and it keeps well for a few days

Great for a summer supper with several people. Goes well with barbequed chicken.
~Ann Pronovost Buckley

Today the group is limited to 12 members who meet 12 times a year and follow one guiding principle, to read widely on an annually chosen theme and then report back to the group in a lengthy essay. Unlike other clubs, these group members need only read one book a year, the one they will explore for the group. The yearly topics often lend themselves to non-fiction and past themes have included the Middle East, indigenous Native Americans, artists and non-American contemporary authors. The meetings are followed by a high tea in the home of the member who is hosting the gathering. Everyone goes home satisfied in both mind and body. It is a special feeling to be part of an organization that has existed for 104 years.

~Sharon Oudemool

Broccoli Salad

Salad Ingredients:
- 5 cups broccoli florets, chopped into small, bite sized pieces
- 8 slices of bacon, cooked crisp and crumbled or ½ c real bacon bits
- ½ cup Craisins or raisins
- ½ cup edamame or frozen peas
- ½ cup sunflower seeds

Salad Dressing
- 1 cup mayo or light mayo
- ¼ cup sugar
- 2 tablespoons white vinegar

Steps:
- In small bowl, combine dressing ingredients until smooth
- Toss salad ingredients in a large bowl
- Pour enough dressing to lightly coat and toss salad
- Chill for a couple of hours before serving
- Toss before serving

Note: All of the add-ins can be adjusted to your preferences. Red onions, scallions or shredded carrot can be added. A store bought creamy poppy seed dressing can be used in place of the above dressing.

This salad was served at the Holiday Luncheon in December 2013 and it was a hit! Originally made to serve 100, this recipe is scaled to a more suitable 8 servings. All quantities can be adjusted to your own preferences.

~Laurie LaConte

CAULIFLOWER SALAD

Ingredients:
- 1 large head of cauliflower, chopped or shredded
- 1½ cups salted peanuts
- 1 (7 ounce) package dried cranberries
- ⅔ cup light mayonnaise
- ⅓ cup sugar

Steps:
- In a large bowl, combine cauliflower, peanuts, cranberries, mayonnaise and sugar. Cover
- Place in the refrigerator for at least one hour before serving
- Stir well before placing on the table
- Note: It can also be made ahead of time

Coming to Cape Cod from Texas, this is for those that can't stand cauliflower. You would never guess that it was the main ingredient. Some people have looked at it and thought it was mashed potato, others whipped cream, but no, it's cauliflower.
~Betsey Stevens

SHOEPEG SALAD

Ingredients:
- 2 (16 ounce) frozen bags white shoepeg corn thawed and drained or 3 cans (11 ounce) white shoepeg corn drained
- 3-4 green onions chopped
- 2-3 celery ribs diced
- 1 small green pepper diced
- 1 English cucumber seeded and chopped
- 1 (16 ounce) bottle of Italian dressing

Steps:
- Prepare a day ahead or at least 8 hours to 10 hours before serving
- Mix together all ingredients except the cucumber
- Add the Italian dressing
- Let marinate in the refrigerator until ready to serve
- Before serving, completely drain the mixture
- Add the chopped cucumber

Note: Leftovers can be saved in the refrigerator up to a week

Serves 10 to 12 but can easily be modified for smaller amounts

A great summer salad to bring to a picnic or a cookout. Pairs well with hot dogs, hamburgers, barbecued back ribs or ham.
~Joan Amodio

BLUEBERRY CAKE
(A Hot Bread)

Ingredients:
- Butter the size of an egg (2 tablespoons+)
- 1 cup sugar
- 1 egg (well beaten if not using electric mixer)
- ½ cup milk
- 2½ cups all-purpose flour
- 1 tablespoon baking powder
- ½ teaspoon salt
- 1 pint blueberries (washed and drained)

Steps:
- Preheat oven to 350°
- Grease and flour a 9 inch square baking pan
- Cream butter and sugar
- Add egg and beat well
- Sift dry ingredients together
- Add dry ingredients alternately with milk. This mixture will be very stiff
- Fold in berries with a spoon.
- Bake 50-60 minutes until top has begun to brown and inserted tester is clean

When we were married, almost 50 years ago, my Aunt gave me a book of family recipes. Over the years this has been our family's favorite. I make and serve it every July 4th immediately after the parade to any family and friends at our house. When asked to bring a family holiday recipe to school, our then 10-year-old grandson made and brought this. Serve warm, cut in squares and split with plenty of butter. You may need a fork!

~Ann Hosmer

Marconi Maritime Center

In 1914, radio pioneer Guglielmo Marconi built a wireless receiving station in Chatham paired with a transmitting station in Marion, Massachusetts, to provide commercial radio service between the United States and Norway. After WWI, the Radio Corporation of America (RCA) put the station into service. Known as Chatham Radio WCC, this was the largest American ship-to-shore station for more than 50 years. Today, the Chatham Marconi Maritime Center (CMMC) leases two 1914 buildings from the Town of Chatham.

Visitors are invited to the Marconi - RCA Wireless Museum in the Operating Building where they will learn about the history of Marconi, Chatham Radio WCC and the U.S. Navy's role in intercepting enemy radio messages during WW II. They will also learn how ship-to-shore messages were sent and received. CMMC's Education Center is next door in the restored Hotel Nautilus. The Center's education initiative focuses on supporting instruction in the fields of science, technology, engineering and mathematics (STEM) in Cape Cod schools and providing a summer program for children.

~Edee Crowell

Lemon Blueberry Bread

Ingredients:
- 1½ cups all-purpose flour
- 1 teaspoon baking powder
- ¼ teaspoon salt
- 6 tablespoons unsalted butter at room temperature
- 1⅓ cups sugar
- 2 large eggs
- ½ cup milk
- 1½ cups fresh blueberries
- 3 tablespoons fresh lemon juice

Steps:
- Preheat oven to 325°
- Butter well or spray with Pam a loaf pan
- Combine first 3 ingredients in small bowl
- Using an electric mixer, cream butter with 1 cup sugar in large bowl until light and fluffy
- Add eggs, 1 at a time, beating well after each addition
- Mix in dry ingredients alternately with milk, beginning and ending with dry ingredients
- Fold in blueberries and spoon batter into prepared loaf pan
- Bake until toothpick inserted into center comes out clean, approximately 1 hour 15 minutes
- While bread bakes, bring remaining ⅓ cup sugar and lemon juice to a boil in small saucepan, stirring until sugar dissolves
- Pierce top of hot bead numerous times with a toothpick and pour hot lemon mixture over loaf in pan
- Cool 30 minutes in pan on a rack
- Turn bread out of pan and cool completely on rack

Makes one 8 inch loaf

A treat with afternoon tea, at breakfast, or as a dessert served with a refreshing sherbet.
~Susan Adsit

Memories of Hurricane Bob

Despite warnings of a huge storm approaching Cape Cod in August 1991, our family of five decided we could surely weather it. This was the last week of our annual Chatham vacation. Our cottage was at the end of Andrew Harding Lane in the Old Village, an ideal location only a few yards from the beach and a quick walk into town. Alas, we could not enjoy our vantage point as the police insisted we seek higher ground and more adequate shelter. The howling winds were terrifying and we were glad to be safe.

After a few hours, the eye passed overhead and it was eerily calm after what had blasted us earlier. When the second half of the storm hit, the wind came at us from the southeast. This caused considerable damage, driving many boats onto the beach and the rock revetments. We returned to find our little cottage mostly intact, but all the leaves had been blown off the trees. Any remaining foliage had turned brown. It was an unusual sight in the middle of the summer.

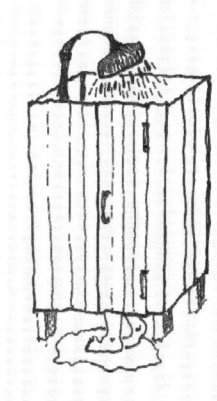

When we ventured out the next day to see the damage, there were many roadblocks due to fallen tree limbs and downed wires everywhere. The storm knocked out power Cape-wide for five days. At first it almost felt like camping but that got old very quickly. As is typical in these types of emergencies, neighbors helped each other. Some had gas lines to stoves and we shared meals. We survivors formed bonds that have lasted to this day.

~Susan Freudenheim

Beach Plum Jelly

Juice Ingredients:
　　8-10 cups beach plums (gather enough beach plums to fill at least half of a one gallon bucket). Use mostly red plums with some purple and some yellow.

Steps to make the juice:
- Rinse beach plums in a colander and discard any brown ones
- Put them in a large pot or kettle and add enough water to almost cover the plums
- Bring to a simmer and cook until soft, approximately 20 minutes
- Mash the plums with a potato masher to release their juice
- Put a jelly bag (or white percale pillowcase) over a large bowl big enough to hold the mash when it is poured
- Set up something from which to hang the jelly bag or pillowcase so the juice will drain into the bowl (we use an old camera tripod)
- Drain overnight. You may gently squeeze the bag to get more juice but it may make the juice cloudier
- Store the juice in a covered container in the refrigerator

Note: you can add more juice as it is made or use the extra to make marinades or syrup

Jelly Ingredients:
　　3½ cups of prepared juice　　2 bars of paraffin
　　6 cups of sugar　　3 ounces of liquid pectin

Steps to make the jelly:
- Sterilize at least 6 jelly glasses by boiling
- Leave in hot water until ready to use
- Melt two bars of paraffin over very low heat and keep warm
- Put the juice, sugar and pectin in a large 8-10 quart pot/kettle and mix well
- Bring above mixture to a boil and boil hard for 1 minute
- Skim off foam. Ladle or pour into prepared jars and top with ⅛ inch paraffin
- Store in a cool dry place. Makes: 6 cups of jelly

Beach Plums are shrubs native to coastal areas from Maine to Virginia. The locations of beach plum thickets are often closely guarded family secrets. This is the Fishback family method of making jelly.
　　　　　　~Sally Fishback

Soups, Salads & More

Atwood House

When Captain Joseph Atwood built his home on Atwood Street in 1752, he had many relatives as neighbors. Today the street is called Stage Harbor Road and the neighbors all have different names. Despite the many changes in Chatham, the original house is unchanged and has become the Atwood House Museum. Captain Atwood would be pleased that his house still stands in its original state and amazed to see the additions to his property.

After you step back into the past with a tour of the old house, there are eight galleries to explore. A few unique features in this old house are the cat door in the keeping room, the view into the root cellar and the portrait of Margery Atwood in her kitchen. There is a model of the salt works in the tool room and a model of a fishing weir in the fishing gallery. The Nickerson Camp was moved from North Beach and is now on the grounds outside. Come for a visit soon and find your own favorite things.

~Marilyn Brown

BRYAN'S FAVORITE PICKLES

Ingredients:
- 6 cups thinly sliced pickling cucumbers (about 2 pounds)
- 2 cups (scant) thinly sliced Vidalia onions
- 1½ cups white vinegar
- ¾ cups sugar
- ¾ teaspoon salt
- ½ teaspoon mustard seeds
- ½ teaspoon celery seeds
- ½ teaspoon ground turmeric
- ½ teaspoon crushed red pepper
- ¼ teaspoon freshly ground black pepper
- 4 garlic cloves, thinly sliced

Steps:
- Place 3 cups cucumbers in a glass bowl
- Top with 1 cup sliced onion
- Repeat with remaining 3 cups cukes and remaining sliced onion
- Combine vinegar and all other ingredients in a small saucepan, stir well
- Bring to a boil. Cook 1 minute
- Pour over cucumbers and onions
- Let cool at room temperature

Note: Cover and chill for three or four days before eating if you can wait that long – otherwise, enjoy right away!

Put all those extra garden cucumbers to good use with this delicious pickle recipe (my nephew's favorite). These add great crunch to summer sandwiches.

~Cece Motz

Historic Plaques

When Chatham celebrated its 300th anniversary in 2012, eleven historic plaques were placed around town from the lighthouse to Ryder's Cove. The eleven plaques are easily accessible and well worth a few hours to search them out and read their interesting contents. The Eldredge Public Library has a guide. Below are some of the historic sites marked with a plaque.

Champlain's Encounter: Samuel de Champlain came to Stage Harbor in 1606 where there was a Wampanoag settlement known as Monomoit. This encounter ended badly with deaths on both sides and the French did not return.

The Mayflower Story at the Lighthouse Overlook: The story of the voyage of the Mayflower is well known to all Americans, but most do not realize that the ship was headed to the Hudson River. On November 9th, 1620 the captain saw the coast of Cape Cod and turned south. About nine miles southeast of Chatham, unable to navigate the shoals of Pollack Rip, the Mayflower turned back and headed north looking for a safe harbor, finding, on November 11th, what is now known as Provincetown Harbor.

Nickerson Family Center: William Nickerson purchased the equivalent of 4,000 acres in 1656 from Monomoyick sachem Mattaquason, in the area we know as Chatham. Two plaques mark the Nickerson Family Center on Orleans Road.

Lighthouse Towers: In 1808 the first two wooden lighthouse towers in Chatham were built. These were replaced by brick structures in 1841 and a plaque at the current single lighthouse notes these changes.

Atwood School: The Doc Keene Scout Hall at the corner of Stage Harbor Road and Cedar Street started life in December of 1839 as a primary school for grades one through four. There were two sessions in the early years. Late November to early March was for boys and they were taught by a male teacher. The summer session began in April and ran through October and was mostly attended by girls who were taught by a female teacher. Both teachers received two dollars a week in compensation, but the man was given two dollars a month for board while the woman received only one dollar.

~Sharon Oudemool

Fish Pier

I love a visit to the fish pier. Dead fish, eager seals waiting for a treat, vigilant seagulls anticipating their chance for food. It is better than an aqua circus. The fishermen go about their business, their catch telling a story of man and sea linked together. I admire their independence and hard work. They are a connection to the past, a long line of seafaring men who braved water and weather to make a living. They don't seem to mind the gawking visitors who peer at them from the deck above.

A dear friend visiting with a new camera requested a trip to the fish pier. The problem was peak season and parking. Waiting behind a white van, I could see no hope for a parking space. My undaunted friend continued to grasp her new camera, pointing to people emerging from the pier. As spaces became available, cars entering from the other direction quickly grabbed them.

Finally the van parked and a woman jumped out. Seeing another space, she sympathetically ran to hold it for me! I was convinced I could not fit into it, but with much cajoling by the woman and her husband and my confident friend, I managed to squeeze into the space.

Needless to say, my friend was ecstatic with her picture-taking opportunities until the battery in her camera died. Oh well, how many seal, seagull and fish photos do you need? I shouldn't have asked. After two more trips to the fish pier, her appetite for photos was at least partially sated. Then, suddenly, seeing that glint in her eye and with camera in hand, she exclaimed, "Let's go to Lighthouse Beach!"

~Pat McKinley

Coastal

Photograph by Margot Karbel

Seafood

Hardings Beach

Where does one find peace, tranquility and relaxation as well as fun? Then add in the ambiance of sand dunes and salty air with an abundance of sea gulls for a picturesque setting. Only two words describe this haven -- Hardings Beach. For the past ten years this place has intrigued me. No matter what season or time of day, Hardings Beach beckons you to its shore.

During the summer months you are surrounded by spectacular views of the Stage Harbor Lighthouse, sail boats, powerboats, swimmers both young and old and kite surfers. One cannot forget the many sea gulls that wait to steal a piece of lunch from unsuspecting visitors. Nantucket Sound's waves, whether gentle or rough, and the motion of the tides provide an opportunity for children to have fun: skimboard, boogie board or watch their sand castles fall into the surf. As winds blow, children gather to fly their kites.

During the off-season, visitors to Hardings Beach are able to see the changes the tides make to the beach. A walk through the dunes during any of the four seasons is a treat for the senses.

It's your memories of the summer fun, however, that will call you back again and again. You can't forget the walks on the beach, the family gatherings and the marvelous views that surround you from sunrise to sunset.

~Lorraine Cocolis

STAGE HARBOR CLAM STEW

Ingredients:
- 3 dozen quahog clams, shucked
- 2 tablespoons butter
- 1 teaspoon celery salt
- 1 teaspoon paprika
- 1 teaspoon Worcestershire sauce
- 1½ cup clam juice
- 3 cups milk

Steps:
- Melt butter
- Blend in celery salt, paprika, Worcestershire sauce
- Pour in clam juice and simmer 2-3 minutes
- Add clams
- As edges curl, add milk
- Bring to boil
- Remove from heat
- Sprinkle with paprika and serve

Serves 4-5

As part of my daughter's wedding celebrations, I served this wonderful stew made with Chatham's treasure, the quahog.
~Gail Tilton

Boat Tours

One reason visitors come to Chatham is for our magnificent waters. With Nantucket Sound, the Atlantic Ocean, the Oyster Pond, Mill Pond and many fresh water ponds, Chatham offers a wide variety of water experiences. One activity that many tourists and residents enjoy is a boat trip to see the seals or a taxi service to North Beach. In 1944, Art Gould began this very popular beach taxi service. Today, the Beachcomber, Chatham Harbor Tours, Rip Ryder and Outermost Harbor Marine offer tourists and residents the chance to spend time on the outer beaches, to see the birds on Monomoy Island or to encounter the seals.

~Ann Hosmer

Oyster Pond Yacht Club

You know that summer is really here when the picnic tables appear in the park at Oyster Pond. For those of us who are fortunate to live on or near Oyster Pond there is an ad hoc potluck supper that somewhat spontaneously happens one night a week during the summer. Come one, come all with a dish in hand. It might be leftovers, something purchased, or a special homemade treat. It is a wonderful way for friends and neighbors to gather and share the news of the week. Years ago this loosely formed group started calling themselves the "Oyster Pond Yacht Club." A burgee was designed and a loosely applied rule was added: you don't need a boat but you can be a little bit dinghy!

~Sally Foster

BOUILLABAISSE

Ingredients:
- 4 medium red potatoes
- 1 pound peeled shrimp
- ½ cup dry white wine
- 1 pound each of cod, halibut & scallops
- 1½ tablespoons tomato paste
- 1½ cup sliced onions
- ½ teaspoon dried thyme
- ¼ cup chopped fresh parsley
- ¼ teaspoon saffron threads (optional)
- 1 tablespoon olive oil
- 2 (8 ounce) bottles clam juice
- ¼ teaspoon salt
- ¼ teaspoon pepper
- 2 lemon slices
- ⅛ fennel bulb
- 1 (14.5 ounce) can of unsalted whole tomatoes, drained
- 2 garlic cloves, minced
- Bay leaf

Steps:
- Microwave potatoes (7-10 minutes) cut into cubes. Don't have them too soft
- Combine all ingredients in a large pot and simmer 25-30 minutes. Discard bay leaf and lemon slices.
- You can use any white fish combination usually use 3 pound total

Flavors blend if prepared several hours in advance

When visiting the Cape on a summer weekend, with all the family we would have Bouillabaisse and warm crusty bread.

~Ann Pronovost Buckley

Seafood

Seafood Cioppino (Stew)

Ingredients:
- 1-2 tablespoons olive oil
- 2-3 cloves garlic, finely chopped
- 1 onion, diced
- 1 cup mushrooms, chopped
- ½ pound hot Italian sausages (2-3 links from the butcher) cut into bite size pieces. You may substitute sweet if you prefer
- Italian seasoning: basil, oregano and thyme (1 teaspoon each)
- 1 jar marinara sauce
- 1 large can of diced tomatoes
- 1 large can peeled plum tomatoes cut in chunks
- 1 pound any white fish (or swordfish), cut up
- ½ pound mussels
- ½ dozen sea scallops
- 8 cherrystone clams
- Lobster meat, squid, shrimp (cleaned) or any other treats from the sea

Steps:
- In a large pot, sauté onion and sausage with olive oil
- Pour off oil if too much
- Add garlic and mushrooms
- Cook a few minutes more at medium heat.
- Add the tomatoes, sauce and Italian seasoning
- Cook until simmering
- Add clams, mussels and fish
- Let this cook on low for about an hour to blend flavors
- Add the scallops and shrimp for about 5-10 minutes
- Serve over pasta or in a bowl with some Italian Bread

Serves 8

When we first moved to Chatham, my sister-in-law taught this recipe to my husband. We used fish that was on sale or caught and created the most delicious meals adding our own shellfish. You can substitute different kinds of fish as a base and it's easy enough that Dad can make it in one pot for the whole family!

~Marilyn Sink

The Monomoyick of Chatham

Have you enjoyed a Cape Cod clambake with friends on the beach, gathered around a sand pit filled with heated rocks, steaming rock seaweed topped with lobsters, clams and corn and covered with a fabric onto which sand is shoveled? This method of cooking a seafood feast, passed down from one generation to the next, came from the Wampanoag.

Archaeological records show Native Americans living in Chatham 9,500-10,000 years ago when Martha's Vineyard and Nantucket were still part of the Cape land mass. The Monomoyick people, who inhabited Chatham at the time of Champlain's visit in 1606, lived in one of 67 villages of Wampanoag extending from the Cape and Islands to southeastern Massachusetts.

The rich history of the Wampanoag in Chatham is complex and complicated for many reasons including poor record keeping, disease and a 1742 Massachusetts law forcing relocation, as well as both official and unofficial discrimination. Native Americans were the last group of people in the United States granted the right to vote in 1924, after this right had previously been given to former slaves and women.

Although there is a strong presence of Native Americans in Chatham today, because of past discriminatory practices, many are unwilling to acknowledge their Native ancestry.

Jill James, a Wampanoag who was born and raised in Chatham, has shared how her Aquinnah Wampanoag grandfather was transferred from the Life Saving Service Station in Aquinnah to Chatham in 1910. He arrived to assume his new position in a suit and tie, not in an Indian headdress of feathers. One of his sons became the first Native American to graduate from the New England Conservatory of Music. The Chatham VFW is named after one of Jill's uncles who died leading a platoon in France in 1944. Jill's father, Howard James, a veteran of the North African campaign in World War II, was a founder of that VFW post and a charter member of the Chatham Band.

One can still see today fishing weirs like those of the Wampanoag in Nantucket Sound, a mishoon, one of their dugout boats at the Atwood House and an often used stone to sharpen tools at Goose Pond.

Fish Stew

Ingredients:
- 1 pound cod
- 1 pound haddock
- 4 potatoes, sliced thinly
- 3 onions, sliced thinly
- A few celery leaves
- 1 bay leaf
- 2½ teaspoons salt
- ¼ teaspoon white pepper
- ½ cup melted butter
- ½ cup vermouth
- ¼ teaspoon dill
- 2 cups light cream
- Paprika
- Fresh parsley

Steps:
- Cut fish into chunks, no skin
- Place on bottom of large casserole
- Layer the potatoes and the onions
- Add celery leaves, bay leaf, salt and pepper
- Melt butter, add vermouth and dill
- Pour over layers
- Bake 1½ hours at 375°
- Slowly heat the cream to a boil
- Pour on top of casserole once it is out of the oven
- Garnish with paprika and fresh parsley

Serves 6-8

This is a favorite recipe from my Mother, Caroline Webster. It has been a favorite with family and friends for three generations now. I hope you get the chance to try it!
~Abigail Doherty

The Chatham Wampanoag Circle, formed to honor the history and presence of the Monomoyick, has published a brochure, Chatham Monomoyick Trail, with maps to historical sites. To learn more about the Wampanoag Program in Chatham contact them at P.O. Box 164, N. Chatham, MA 02650.

~Eve Dalmolen

Fantastic Fish Pie

Ingredients:
- 5 large potatoes peeled, diced into 1 inch squares
- 2 hard boiled eggs, cooled and cut into quarters
- 2 large handfuls of spinach or kale
- 1 onion, finely chopped
- 1 carrot, finely chopped
- Extra virgin olive oil
- 1½ cups heavy cream
- 3 cups of grated sharp cheddar & Gruyère cheese combined
- Juice of one lemon
- 1 heaping teaspoon of Dijon mustard
- 1 handful of flat-leaf parsley finely chopped (can use 1 tablespoon dried)
- 1 pound cod, cut in chunks
- ½ pound shrimp, peeled and deveined
- ½ pound sea scallops, cut in pieces
- ½ cup Greek yogurt or sour cream
- Salt and freshly ground pepper

Steps:
- Boil potatoes in salted water until tender
- Steam the spinach or kale in a steamer
- Cook the onion and carrot in a small amount of olive oil for about five minutes or until tender
- Add 1 cup of cream to the onions and carrots. Heat until boiling and remove from heat
- Mix the lemon, parsley, mustard and 2 cups of the cheese into the cream mixture
- When potatoes and spinach are done, drain the spinach and squeeze out any excess water
- Put the potatoes in a bowl to mash
- Butter the bottom of a 13 x 9 inch pan
- Put the fish, shrimp and scallops, spinach/kale and eggs into the pan. Pour the cream mixture over it
- Add extra ½ cup of cream if necessary to make sauce creamy
- Mash the potatoes adding salt and pepper, the yogurt or sour cream and the extra virgin olive; taste and adjust the seasoning - I often add more yogurt
- Mix in the rest of the cheese
- Spoon and lightly spread the potatoes over the fish mixture. Dot with butter
- You can prepare to this point and put it in the refrigerator until about 10 minutes before cooking
- Bake in preheated oven at 450° degrees for 30 minutes – until the potatoes are golden and bubbling

Serves 8

My family loves it. Great for company. I always get rave reviews. Good with fresh steamed asparagus or a nice green salad and homemade bread.

~Gail Smith

A Glorious Day of Boating

It was one of those days: idyllic summer temperatures, bright sunshine and a slight breeze. We had to get on the water. About noon we embarked from Ryder's Cove and set out for Pleasant Bay. The views of Eastward Ho! Golf Course did not disappoint and our son and daughter-in-law were duly impressed. After tying up at a mooring by the Chatham Yacht Club (CYC), we unfolded the deck chairs and enjoyed sandwiches. An added bonus was watching the CYC race-school students "feel the wind" in their 420s while the afternoon course was being set.

We let loose from the mooring ball and set out for the north cut. I'm not sure what made me set the fishing line on this short pleasure cruise, but lo and behold, we had a hit and boated a striper. It was a keeper.

Continuing on to the main entry, the vista of the lighthouse and the beach area around it was awesome. Several seals even provided us an escort. We stayed close to shore, enjoying the view of Chatham Bars Inn, and passed under the elevators at the fish pier. Rounding Minister's Point, we reached our marina.

How to cook this beautiful, fresh fish was now the focus. Our family provided the answers after an internet search. We purchased condiments from the local stores, made a green salad, chilled the Chardonnay and set the table on the deck. The striper was roasted with lemon, lime and white wine. Our dinner complemented a delightful day spent on the water.

~Elaine Pfeifer

Kayaking

Nearly a decade ago, we bought our first two kayaks. We enjoyed them so much that we now own a fleet. We have discovered many waterways throughout the Cape but have always liked those close to home best. Our favorite kayak adventure, which we do at least once a summer, is the four-mile trip from Mill Pond to Oyster Pond Beach. We often put in at Bridge Street and paddle under the historic Mitchell River Bridge and past the many fishing boats, sailboats and yachts moored in Stage Harbor. Sometimes we see a sailing class from the local yacht club practicing their maneuvers.

We pass the Stage Harbor entrance to Nantucket Sound and begin the long trip down the Oyster River. If we have timed our day correctly, we are able to paddle along with the incoming tide. We see many homes that, from the land, are hidden by long driveways but give us great views from the water. Some are small cottages that cling to the water's edge. Others are huge and look ready for a large gathering.

When we paddle by the oyster beds, we remember why the pond got its name. Sometimes there are lots of boats passing by and we greet each other with a friendly wave. As we enter Oyster Pond, we always stop paddling to take time to appreciate the picture perfect postcard view of Chatham with its three church steeples. We often hear the sounds of children laughing and playing at the beach. But the best part of the trip is knowing that we live here.

~Deborah Clark and Sue Simpson

Coquilles Saint Jacques

Ingredients:
- 8 ounces button mushrooms, minced
- 6 tablespoons unsalted butter
- 3 small shallots, minced
- 2 tablespoons minced parsley
- Kosher salt and freshly ground black pepper, to taste
- ¾ cup dry white wine
- 1 bay leaf
- 6 large sea scallops
- 2 tablespoons flour
- ½ cup heavy cream
- ⅔ cup grated Gruyère cheese
- ½ teaspoon fresh lemon juice

Steps:
- Heat mushrooms, 4 tablespoons butter and ⅔ of the minced shallots in a 4 quart saucepan over medium heat; cook until the mixture forms a loose paste, about 25 minutes
- Stir parsley into mushroom mixture; season with salt and pepper
- Divide mixture among 6 cleaned scallop shells or shallow gratin dishes
- Bring remaining shallots, wine, bay leaf, salt and ¾ cup water to a boil in a 4 quart saucepan over medium heat
- Add scallops; cook until barely tender, about 2 minutes
- Remove scallops; place each over mushrooms in shells
- Continue boiling cooking liquid until reduced to ½ cup, about 10 minutes; strain
- Heat broiler to high
- Heat remaining butter in a 2 quart saucepan over medium heat. Add flour; cook until smooth, about 2 minutes
- Add reduced cooking liquid and cream; cook until thickened, about 8 minutes
- Add cheese, lemon juice, salt and pepper; divide the sauce over scallops
- Broil until browned on top, about 3 minutes

Serves 6

To honor the venerable Chatham Scallop - one of my favorite ways to enjoy sea scallops!

~Margot Karbel

CHATHAM HALF SHELL MUSSELS NEOPOLITAN

Ingredients:
- 3 pounds mussels
- 3 tablespoons olive oil
- 1 large clove garlic
- 6 ounces tomato paste
- ½ teaspoon oregano
- 1-2 tablespoons capers, rinsed
- ¼ teaspoon crushed red pepper

Steps to cook mussels:
- Clean mussels and remove beards
- Steam mussels in 1 cup water until opened
- Place mussels on the half shell and arrange in a shallow baking pan
- Strain and reserve the mussel liquor; add water if needed to equal 2½ cups

Steps to make sauce:
- Heat the oil in a saucepan
- Sliver the garlic lengthwise and brown in the oil
- Add the tomato paste and sauté for 2 minutes with garlic
- Add mussel liquor, oregano and rinsed capers
- Simmer, covered, for about 30 minutes
- Add crushed red pepper
- Pour sauce over the mussels and bake in preheated 425° oven for 15 minutes or until hot
- Serve with sliced, toasted Italian bread.

Serves: 4 as an appetizer or multiply as a main course over pasta but don't exceed ½ teaspoon of red pepper.

Note: The sauce freezes well.

This seafood treat is always a big hit! Can be prepared in advance and heated for serving.

~Pat Vreeland

United States Coast Guard Auxiliary

The United States Coast Guard Auxiliary, USCGA, is the uniformed volunteer component of the United States Coast Guard (USCG) that exists to support all USCG missions except those requiring law enforcement or military engagement.

At the Chatham-based flotilla, an auxiliarist may find him or herself involved in any number of activities. Teaching boating safety to the general public is popular. Conducting search and rescue of stranded vessels and safety examinations of commercial fishing vessels and recreational boats are vital services of the auxiliary. Monitoring aids to navigation such as buoys, lighthouses and fog signals is another task. Tours of the Chatham Lighthouse are under the direction of the local auxiliary.

Chatham Flotilla 11-1 is proud to partner with the USCG assigned to Station Chatham, conducting several events each year in support of the local unit and its families.

~Ruth Tichenor

MUSSELS DIJON

Ingredients:
  4 pounds mussels, rubbed and scrubbed
  1 tablespoon chopped garlic
  1 tablespoon chopped shallots
  1 carrot, grated
  1 scallion stalk, diced
  2 ounces clarified butter
  3 ounces white wine
  2 teaspoons Dijon mustard
  ¾ cups heavy cream

Steps:
- Place butter (or part olive oil) in large kettle, turn on high
- Add garlic, shallots, carrots and scallions
- Sauté until wilted
- Add wine and reduce by a quarter
- Add mustard, cream and mussels
- Cover pot and shake to cover mussels with sauce. Steam until the mussels open

Note: Great served with crusty bread and a salad
Serves 4

Mussels are in abundance in Chatham so it's an easy dish to create.
~Robin Zibrat

OYSTERS & CORN CASSEROLE

Ingredients:
- 1 quart oysters
- 2 eggs, beaten
- 2 cans creamed corn
- 2 cups crushed saltine crackers

Steps:
- Drain oysters well.
- Mix oysters, corn and crackers.
- Add beaten eggs, mix well
- Put into greased casserole dish.
- Bake at 350° for 35-40 minutes until bubbly and firm

Serves: 6

Great holiday side dish!
Quick and easy.
~Kathleen Read

Shorebirds and Waterfowl

Chatham is surrounded on three sides by water -- Nantucket Sound to the south, the Atlantic Ocean to the east and Pleasant Bay to the north. Along the town's nearly 66 mile shoreline, there are barrier beaches, marshes, tidal rivers, inlets and estuaries that become excellent feeding grounds for migrant shorebirds and form protected waters for winter waterfowl. The beach grasses and thickets along the dunes and the nearby upland are yearlong habitat for a great number of species.

Each season there are wonderful birding opportunities and people with binoculars and spotting scopes are a regular sight. A walk along the coast in the spring might yield a

Sea Scallops with Lemon~Butter Sauce

Ingredients:
- 1 cup rice
- 1½ teaspoon salt
- ¼ teaspoon pepper
- 1½ cup shredded baby spinach
- 1 pound sea scallops
- 2 tablespoons flour
- 2 tablespoons olive oil
- 4 tablespoons butter
- 2 tablespoons parsley, chopped
- 1 tablespoon lemon juice

Steps:
- Cook rice, following package directions, adding 1 teaspoon salt and shredded baby spinach for last 3 minutes of cooking
- Coat sea scallops in flour
- Season with ¼ teaspoon salt and ⅛ teaspoon pepper
- Sauté scallops in 2 tablespoons olive oil and 2 tablespoons butter in large skillet over high heat 2 minutes on each side. Remove scallops
- Add 2 tablespoons butter, lemon juice, chopped parsley, ¼ teaspoon salt, ⅛ teaspoon pepper and stir
- Serve scallops over rice and top with sauce from skillet

Makes 4 servings

~Donna Lepri

---

view of American Oystercatchers with their bright red beaks. In the late summer Willets, Dunlin and Sanderling can be found chasing the edges of the incoming waves. Ruddy Turnstones pop along hunting with their feet in the rack line. During the winter Goldeneyes, Mergansers, Loons and occasionally Harlequin Ducks can be found swimming and diving in the nearby waters. Horned Larks, Snow Buntings or even a rare sighting of a Snowy Owl turns a winter day into an exciting moment.

The shores of Chatham and the Monomoy Wildlife Refuge are considered to be premiere birding destinations for viewing shorebirds and ducks along the North Atlantic coast.

~Joanna Schurmann

Schoolhouse Pond Memories

My parents built our present home on Schoolhouse Pond in 1986. It was a summer home with occasional winter visits for us all. The first time I saw the house it was only framed and I was seven months pregnant. I carefully climbed the long flight of stairs to explore this work in progress. Most of my attention, however, was focused on the gorgeous view of the pond.

In 2012, coinciding with the 300th birthday of Chatham, we became full-time residents. Much has changed over the years. My parents are both gone and my children are grown. They do come back, along with lots of their friends. And I can feel my parents in these rooms every day. I can see the pond from every room in my home and, whether the water is frozen or cobalt blue, cold or warm, I think of my parents and miss them. I also think of my children - swimming, laughing, kayaking, paddle boarding on the pond, digging in the sand and building castles in the sun when they were younger.

As I walk on the beach around Schoolhouse Pond it is full of memories - past and present, lovely and poignant. I look forward to creating more memories as future generations enjoy the natural beauty of the pond for many years to come.

~Rosanne Geylin

BAKED FINNAN HADDIE

Ingredients:
- 2 pounds smoked haddock fillets
- 2 tablespoons all-purpose flour
- ¼ cup melted butter
- 2 cups warm milk

Steps:
- Preheat oven to 325°
- Place smoked haddock into a glass baking dish
- Whisk flour into melted butter until smooth
- Then whisk in milk
- Pour over haddock
- Bake about 35 minutes or until sauce has thickened and fish flakes off easily

Serves 6

My husband's Scottish Great Aunt came to Massachusetts from Nova Scotia in the early 1900s and brought this old family recipe. She was a fabulous "scratch" cook - hardly ever a measurement, so you had to watch carefully. Great with mashed potatoes and veggie!

~Ann Wade

Lovers Lake

Could the two mating swans, nicknamed Romeo and Juliet, be the reason Lovers Lake got its name? Originally called Lords Pond, Lovers Lake is the only lake in Chatham; all the other bodies of water are called ponds. My husband first came here in the late 1950s. He remembers tubing, boating, sailing and fishing on this beautiful glacier formed kettle pond as well as being chased by an otter while paddling on his inner tube. Now there is limited public access from town owned land (Chatham Conservation Foundation managed) on its north side where canoes or kayaks can be portaged in for fishing or swimming.

Technically, calling this body of water a lake is a misnomer as it is smaller (38 acres) than ponds in the area. Because its size is over 10 acres, it is classified as a "Great Pond" and is owned by the Commonwealth in public trust. This kettle pond was formed by the ground sinking as the glacier's ice melted and the area filling with rain and ground water. Its maximum depth is 36 feet with an average depth of 15 feet. The lake's overflow spills into Stillwater Pond and then into Pleasant Bay. There is a small herring run between Stillwater Pond and Lovers Lake at the north end.

On May 12, 2013, there was quite a surprise for all the lake homeowners. A small plane had to make an emergency landing on the lake. You often see them flying over the lake in their flight pattern from the nearby local airport; however, none has ever actually landed in it before. You never know what visitors will show up on this lake!!

~Diane Karel

A Day at the Beach

If you have a house in Chatham, you will have guests.
Guests love to go to the beach!!
Our gorgeous beaches have their own character and charm.
Here is how we do it:

We gather and collect all the necessities:
Beach towels
Beach chairs
Beach books & Kindles
Beach umbrella
Sunglasses and sunscreen (lots of it!)
Cooler filled with drinks, sandwiches and chips
Games like beach pong, lacrosse, frisbee and kites
Buckets, pails, shovels and baggies for shells
AND a camera to record the fun!!

Then, after shoving all this in the car and piling in, we find a willing driver to drop us off.
We arrive smeared with lotion in our bathing suits, having been sliding on the car seats on the way.
After immediately kicking off our shoes, we traipse through the sand lugging all the equipment.
We find the perfect spot, setting the chairs to promote conversation and sun worship.
We laugh and talk and watch the games and cool off in the water.
Babies sleep protected by ingenious set-ups of chairs, towels and contraptions.
The end of the day arrives too quickly before we head home to the outdoor shower.
Wet feet make paths through the house...another perfect summer day at the beach!!

In September, when all the guests are gone, here is how we go to the beach:
We drive to the beach and pick our favorite spot.
We set up our chairs that live in our trunk all year round.
We sit there quietly in the cool sand remembering the lovely summer days with family and friends.
We meet old friends and share our summer stories.
AND, for one last time, we wiggle our toes in the sand.

~Madonna Hitchcock

COMPANY FISH

Ingredients:
- 4 (8 ounce) fish filets such as sole
- Kosher salt and freshly ground black pepper
- 8 ounces crème fraiche
- 3 tablespoons Dijon mustard
- 1 tablespoon whole-grain mustard
- 2 tablespoons minced shallots
- 2 teaspoons drained capers

Steps:
- Preheat oven to 425°
- Line a sheet pan with parchment paper or use an oven proof baking dish
- Place fish fillets skin side down on the sheet pan
- Sprinkle generously with salt and pepper
- Combine the crème fraiche, 2 mustards, shallots, capers, 1 teaspoon salt and ½ teaspoon pepper in a small bowl
- Spoon the sauce evenly over the fish fillets, making sure the fish is completely covered
- Bake for 10-15 minutes, depending on the thickness of the fish, until it's barely done. Be sure not to overcook it

Note: The fish will flake easily at the thickest part when it's done

Serve hot or at room temperature with the sauce from the pan spooned over the top

Delicious and easy to make!
~Susan Turner Pinzuti

<u>Fish Recipe</u>
Catch fish
Clean fish
Cook fish
Eat fish

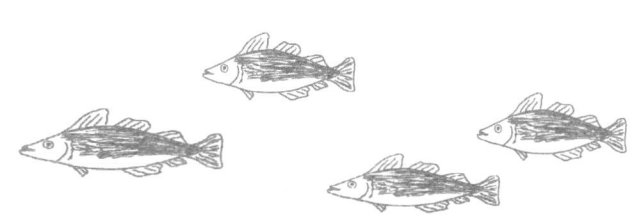

Chatham Bars Inn (CBI)

Celebrating its hundred year anniversary, our local resort is a business that is woven into the fabric of Chatham. With gorgeous views of the harbor and the barrier beach beyond, CBI is renowned for the activities we Chatham residents enjoy every day: boating, swimming in the Atlantic Ocean, bicycling the loop, fishing, walking the town to shop, playing golf and tennis, relaxing at the spa and enjoying clambakes.

Charles Hardy built the resort in 1914 with 50 rooms, a golf course, a pool, a farm and a wooden bridge to North Beach. He also built the Brick Block in town. Later he financed the development of Eastward Ho! Golf Course as well. The resort, the town and the activities work very well together and attract thousands each summer. The inn has kept true to its style of 1914. They have antique woodie cars and trolleys to transport guests to town and on tours. A special centennial celebration event was an ice cream social open to the public, repeating the original opening event of 1914.

One winter day a few years ago, a TV morning show did a segment on the summer jobs their anchors had. Diane Sawyer worked at CBI as a waitress in her college days. Shortly thereafter, she showed up in Chatham to make a video of herself performing waitressing duties at CBI's main dining room. With the capable instruction of one of CBI's best waiters, she had fun being a waitress again and reminiscing about the great summer she had working with her college classmates. It made pretty good TV!!!

~Regina McDowell

HONEY MUSTARD GLAZED SALMON

Ingredients:
  2 tablespoons fresh lemon juice
  2 tablespoons Dijon mustard
  2 tablespoons honey
  4 (5 ounce) salmon fillets

Steps:
- In an oiled shallow baking dish, combine lemon juice, Dijon mustard and honey. Mix together. Add salmon
- Flip salmon to coat in glaze
- Bake immediately or cover with plastic wrap and refrigerate for up to 3 hours
- When ready to cook, preheat oven to 400°
- Bake 20 minutes or until fish is fork-tender

Serves 4

"Amazing and healthy!" It is quick and easy to make.

~Betsy Bray

SESAME BROILED SALMON WITH WASABI MARINADE

Ingredients:
- 1 tablespoon sesame seeds
- 2 tablespoons wasabi powder (such as McCormack's)
- 1 tablespoon water
- 1 tablespoon low sodium soy sauce
- 2 tablespoons olive oil
- 2 tablespoons rice wine vinegar
- 1 tablespoon light brown sugar
- 1½ pound salmon filet, cut into 6 servings

Steps:
- Toast sesame seeds over medium high heat in non-stick skillet for 3 minutes until light golden brown
- Mix wasabi powder, water and soy sauce in a small bowl
- Add oil, vinegar, brown sugar and sesame seeds. Mix well
- Reserve 2 tablespoons of marinade for basting later
- Place salmon and marinade in a zip top plastic bag and turn to coat
- Marinate at room temperature for 30 minutes. Remove the salmon and discard marinade
- Place salmon on rack of broiling pan (fold thin ends of salmon under for more even cooking)
- Broil 8 – 10 minutes per inch of thickness to desired doneness
- Brush it with reserved marinade the last 2 minutes

~Kathie Curran

The Veranda

With high anticipation my three friends and I gathered for lunch on the Veranda at Chatham Bars Inn. Since we all came from sunny mornings at our Cape homes, it was a bit of a let down to see the fog roll in over the Chatham bars. We weren't able to watch the boats come into the fishing pier. I was disappointed because I had so often described the colorful, peaceful view from the Veranda.

While we sipped our iced tea and munched on our delicious salads, nature had a surprise for us. Gradually the gray shoreline changed before our eyes. The fog quietly lifted. Not only could we see some of the fishing fleet, we could also see the cottages on the outer beach. The water sparkled shades of blue and green, striated with pale brown sand. "Now," said one of my friends, "I see why they call them the 'Chatham bars'."

~Alayne Tsigas

Seafood

Broiled Oriental Swordfish

Ingredients:
- 2 tablespoons lemon juice
- 2 tablespoons soy sauce
- 1 tablespoon olive oil
- 1 tablespoon minced ginger
- 1 clove garlic, minced
- ½ pound swordfish steak, cut 1½ inches thick
- Vegetable oil for broiling dish
- 1 scallion, thinly sliced on diagonal
- 1 lemon, cut in half

Steps:
- Combine lemon juice, soy sauce, olive oil, ginger and garlic in bowl
- Marinate fish in mixture for 1 hour in the refrigerator, turning occasionally
- Remove from marinade and scrape off any ginger or garlic that clings
- Strain marinade, reserving liquid
- Preheat broiler
- Place swordfish 4 inches from heat source on a lightly oiled flat broiling dish. (Do not place fish directly on broiling rack, which can break it apart). Fish can also be cooked on outdoor grill
- Brushing with reserved marinade, broil fish to desired degree of doneness (4 to 5 minutes per side)
- Sprinkle with scallion and garnish with lemon halves

Serves 2

~Donna Lepri

Sharks

Since the movie "Jaws" was released, people have been terrified of great white sharks. That is, people who don't live in Chatham! Here we have embraced them—well not literally! In 1972 grey seals became protected in United States waters. Because the seals are here, sharks have seasonally migrated to Chatham's waters. Every summer for the last few years sharks have shown up off Lighthouse Beach and off Orleans and Truro. Scientists have also arrived here to tag these large denizens of the ocean and track their migratory routes.

To celebrate the sharks, in 2013 a contest was held at Kate Gould Park entitled "Sharks in the Park," where local businesses and organizations decorated plastic PVC sharks with a myriad of designs. These were auctioned off at the conclusion of this festival. The great whites have put Chatham on the map. During the summer the network news often comes to Lighthouse Beach to report on the sharks. The Discovery Channel even included Chatham in "Shark Week" in 2010 and 2012. Shark souvenirs are sold in Chatham stores. Because most beaches in Chatham are not located near shark territory, swimming and tourists have not been adversely affected. Now each summer when the sharks return for their "seal-meal," Chatham is once again in the news. Curiosity has drawn many visitors to our town in hopes of seeing a great white.

~Mary Ann Chamberlain

Swordfish or Tuna
~Olives, Capers, Peppers & Tomato~

Ingredients:
- 3 tablespoons extra-virgin olive oil
- 3 large cloves garlic, thinly sliced
- ½ cup red onions, thinly sliced
- 1¼ to 1½ pound swordfish, tuna, or other dark fleshed fish, skinned and cut into 1 inch wide strips
- 1 tablespoon minced fresh basil
- 1 tablespoon minced fresh mint
- 1 teaspoon minced fresh oregano or marjoram
- Salt and pepper to taste
- 1 cup chopped, seeded, peeled tomatoes, fresh or canned
- 1 tablespoon capers, drained
- ¼ cup Gaeta, Kalamata, or other good dark olives, pitted if you like
- Red pepper flakes

Steps:
- Heat olive oil and garlic in a large skillet over low heat until the garlic turns pale gold, 15 to 20 minutes
- Remove the garlic with a slotted spoon to a small bowl. Increase the heat to medium-high and add the thinly sliced red onions
- Cook for about 2 minutes. Add fish
- Increase the heat to high and quickly sear the fish on all sides, while seasoning it with basil, mint, oregano (or marjoram). Salt and pepper to taste
- Cook until the fish is done to your liking, 2-5 minutes
- Remove the fish to a hot platter or warm oven
- Return the garlic to the skillet along with tomatoes, olives and capers and add pinch of red pepper flakes
- Cook for just a minute, stirring occasionally. Spoon over the fish
- Garnish with basil and mint

Only strong tasting fish such as swordfish, tuna, bluefish, or king mackerel can stand up to this highly spiced sauce from the Italian region of Calabria. Use the best olives that you can find - they will make a difference.

~Ella Leavitt

North Beach

North Beach is a barrier beach which spans 10 miles from Orleans to Chatham. It protects the coastline of Chatham from the Atlantic Ocean. North Beach was originally used to harvest salt hay and had several hunting shacks amid the dunes. It was a favorite among duck hunters and has been the site of many shipwrecks.

North Beach became a destination for campers, boaters and beach camp owners over the years. The Chatham end was divided by two "villages," north and south. It was a great escape to live on the beach, enjoy the fishing, clamming and surfing. Day tripping by boat or buggy was the alternative to staying in a camp or camper and was enjoyed by many.

Entrance onto the beach by beach buggy was at Nauset Beach in Orleans. The drive down the entire length ended just across from Morris Island. The "cut" was then located between North Beach and Monomoy Island. This was the entrance to Chatham Harbor. Boats would enter there between the buoys. It was often very rough to enter the harbor. The wreckage of the Pendleton in the distance was a constant reminder of what could happen. At this time the beach was so wide we could drive on "outer" beach, the "elephant road" which was over the dunes, the inside road which was by the bay, or the low beach at low tide. It was quite a walk to go from the bay side to the Atlantic.

Many cottages were built in the late 1950s, when several tracts of land were sold by George Bearse. Floating the wood over on barges, using battleship bunk beds for beds, bringing a wood stove, a gas stove, gas lights and refrigerator provided all the comforts of home. Water was pumped into the sink from a hand dug well. Everything had to be lugged to the beach. It was a meeting spot for family parties, clambakes, vacations and quiet times. It was a community of camp owners who shared their love of the beach. Camp dwellers would commute to work in the summer by boat.

Over the years there has been controversy over the ownership of the beach. In 1958 the federal government under the newly instituted National Seashore "bought" most of Chatham's privately owned land on North Beach. There was hardly a choice and those with building permits issued prior to 1958 were grandfathered. Those after were allowed to use their camp for a leased fee for 25 more years, until the beach could be brought back to its original condition.

Over the course of many years the beach has changed and eroded. In 1977 the Coast Guard Station was moved to Provincetown before it could collapse into the sea. Many of the camps on the ocean and bay side were lost to storms such as the blizzard of 1978. In 1987, a ferocious storm hit the elbow of Cape Cod and tore the beach in half causing a "break" in front of the Chatham Lighthouse. This brought considerable changes to the harbor, local town landings and beach front homes. Erosion became the town's worst nightmare pitting the homeowner against the Conservation Commission and the State to try and save their property. In the end many homes were lost to the sea. The channels were constantly changing and redirecting. Navigation was difficult. We now have North and South Beach.

In 1991, the storm known as the "No-Name Storm" crashed into our shores on a dark Halloween night and again devastated our shoreline and properties. The day before, standing at the Cow Yard, it appeared our camp was bouncing. Waves could be seen breeching the beach; then darkness came. The next day as the fog rose we saw a flat wasteland. Beach camps from North Beach had floated across the harbor and were found scattered along the shoreline. This storm took a huge amount of the beach out to sea. The land was flat, dunes disappeared and new channels began to take shape. Clam flats disappeared.

Many of the lost camps still had years remaining on their government leases and were rebuilt. Still enjoying the wonders of the beach, we rebuilt our cottage on stilts according to FEMA regulations, instead of nestled in the dunes made of driftwood and old doors. The new "shacks" became camps with even more modern adornments. Some were wired for generators and solar energy. They sat on pilings well above the dunes. The ride down the beach was no longer three or four roads; it now was two roads - inside or outside. Many times the roads were flooded and difficult to drive. With the erosion came the loss of many dunes and the beach became very narrow and flat in places. The plovers arrived to nest on our beaches.

In 2006, another storm struck. This storm devastated the North Village and wiped out most of the camps. It also broke a new cut in the beach. Part of North Beach, from Minister's Point to the lighthouse, was now an island. The "South Village" could no longer be accessed by buggy. This made navigation into the harbor, entering at both ends of the beach, difficult. The harbor continued to change and there was even more beach erosion. It also meant the only way to the camps was by boat. No longer could you drive the gas tanks, food and supplies down the beach. Everything had to be lugged and delivered by boat. This limited the access during the late fall and winter months. No longer could you ride down for Thanksgiving, Christmas or on a brisk March night.

In 2011 the National Seashore decided the remaining "leased" camps would have to be removed for navigational purposes. The long and hard fight to retain most of the beloved camps ended when they were dismantled in March 2012.

Two were demolished in September 2014. Now only two camps remain. The beach is the narrowest it's been in 100 years. We still enjoy the small spit of land for day trips but only Mother Nature knows for how long. It's forever changing and a way of life is gone. The barrier beaches threaten to be no barrier at all.

~Robin Zibrat

Community

Photograph by Eunice Geist

Meats & Poultry

Chatham Band Concerts

For over 80 years, on every Friday evening in summer – weather permitting – the heart of downtown Chatham comes alive with the music of the Chatham Band performing their magic in Kate Gould Park. Yes, magic. From the flautist to the bass drummer, each musician brings his or her own piece of the melody, harmony or rhythm to the stage of the Whit Tileston Bandstand. Under the skillful baton of the conductor, the band comes together to create something that does not exist without each other – a patriotic song, a wonderful waltz, the Bunny Hop! Children march and sing around the bandstand, grandparents dance with their grandchildren and couples waltz to the music. And after the last selection is played, the magic disperses through the streets as families make their way home, still humming a tune and sometimes gazing at the moon. Music. Magic. Memories.

~Paula Lofgren

CHICKEN DIVAN

Ingredients:
- 4 cups cooked broccoli florets
- 1½ cups cooked chicken, cubed
- 1 can cream of mushroom soup
- ⅓ cup milk
- ½ cup cheddar cheese, shredded
- ¼ cup dry seasoned bread crumbs
- 1 tablespoon butter

Steps:
- Layer chicken and broccoli in baking dish
- Combine soup and milk
- Pour over chicken and broccoli
- Sprinkle with cheese
- Top with bread crumbs and dot with butter
- Bake in 350° oven for 20 minutes

A great quick recipe I use for family and company.
~Lorraine Cocolis

Monomoy Theater

An enjoyable summer activity is attending the Monomoy Theater. For over fifty years, the Ohio University School of Theater sponsored the summer program. In 2012, the University of Hartford became a partner and will continue this theater tradition.

The season always starts with a well-known musical and continues with a different play each week until the end of August, with a variety of drama and comedy and one Shakespearean play. I continually marvel at the way a student can portray the lead one week while rehearsing for another role in the next play. Not only does the Monomoy Theater give students training in drama, but there are opportunities for many behind-the-scenes workers to build the beautiful stage settings, work the lights and even take a turn at weeding the garden or parking cars.
~Eunice Geist

Chicken Picatta

Ingredients:

- 2½ pounds thin chicken cutlets (slice each breast in half)
- ½ teaspoon salt
- ¼ teaspoon pepper
- 1 cup Wondra flour
- 3 tablespoons olive oil
- 3 tablespoons butter
- ½ cup dry white wine
- 2 cups chicken broth
- 1 lemon, sliced thin
- 2 tablespoons capers
- 2 tablespoons chopped parsley

Steps:
- Dredge chicken in salt, pepper and Wondra flour
- Heat olive oil and butter in a large pan (electric frying pan works well)
- Sauté 3 minutes per side or until brown
- Remove and keep warm
- To the skillet add butter and olive oil (1 tablespoon each)
- Add 2 tablespoons Wondra flour to the mix and cook 1 minute
- Add the wine to deglaze the pan and to scrape up any browned bits
- Reduce wine by half (about 30 seconds)
- Add chicken broth and lemon and simmer 2 minutes or until sauce is thick
- Add chicken – simmer 5 minutes
- Add capers and garnish with parsley

This recipe is great for dinner parties. It can be made in the morning and then reheated before serving.
~Rita Broman

Downtown Chatham Living

Around the turn of the new century, we moved from the outskirts of town into Chatham village within an easy walk of Main Street and its many enticements. Our extended family came to love this new location because they could visit so many places without having to use a vehicle. On lazy summer mornings everyone can take their time getting ready for that day's adventures. Those who are restless need not sit around and wait for the others; they can walk in one direction and take a dip in Oyster Pond at the town beach or take a short walk in the other direction and browse through Ben Franklin or visit the Candy Manor or Buffy's Ice Cream. When our grandchildren have been asked their favorite spot in Chatham, they often can't decide between the cooling effects of water fun or the warming effects of sweets in their tummies.

~Sally Foster

Retail on Main Street

For over half a century the place to go in Chatham to buy a bright blue windbreaker for your days on the water in your sparkling white boat was 482 Main Street, home of Mark, Fore and Strike. Shoppers would delight in the bright, resort-type clothes with the names most popular at any given time. Working in the store for nearly ten years, I helped many men and women find just the right cheery, vibrant and colorful apparel for Cape Cod life.

In 1986 there was a fire in the building but soon a remodeled 482 Main Street was up and running. Sadly, the company went out of business in early 2008. Soon after, another company opened in the same spot. It is a privately owned company whose owner also enjoys being on or very near to the ocean.

Working at Mark, Fore and Strike on Main Street was fun, exciting and gave me an opportunity to meet people from all over the world!

~Janet McGuigan

Eldredge Public Library

My feet were wet, my nose was red
And snow was piled upon my head.

I pulled upon the mighty door
And entered dripping on the floor.

To the desk I went and said in glee
"Tis April, how can this weather be?"

She answered "Tis Spring!
The New England way!
So come on in and have a stay."

So I searched the stacks and chose a book.
Then found myself a cozy nook.

In the room with a fireplace and a comfy chair
Sat myself down and stayed right there.

For the rest of the day through snow, then rain
Sloshing on colored window pane

I lost myself in the gift of story
And reveled in the presence of all this glory.

A library filled with subtle power
To give sustenance for many an hour

To mind and body, spirit and soul...
Perhaps that is its very goal!

May it always be this special place
A building with a human face.

That beckons and welcomes and comforts, too.
That's what our library can do for you.
                           ~Pat McKinley

Eldredge Public Library

The Eldredge Public Library is one of the most frequently utilized buildings in Chatham. Over 10,000 visitors are welcomed by our dedicated staff each year. There are programs for all ages, from Itsy Bitsy Yoga, to story hours for children and gatherings for youth and tweens. Book and Author sessions are widely popular and are offered year round. The Friends of the Library offer a variety of courses in its Learning Series in both the Fall and Winter/Spring. Free WIFI and computers are available. If you love history, you'll delight in the stained glass windows and warm paneling of the reading room. For ancestry buffs, there are genealogical resources. And, if you are home bound, free delivery of books and materials is available. Something for everyone; that's our library treasure!

~Phyllis Freeman

South Chatham Library

You will find this unique library is a gem in South Chatham. Located at the corner of Main Street (Rt.28) and Mill Creek Road, it is a small one room library, one of the few remaining private libraries in the United States. Do not let its size fool you for its shelves contain over 3,000 books, many of which are current fiction and non-fiction bestsellers. While videos and DVDs are not purchased by the library, they do loan out those which have been donated. Do not look for a computer at check-out time. It is the old-fashioned card system. Open on Tuesdays and Fridays from 1-4 pm throughout the year, residents, non-residents and vacationers are welcomed. There is a friendly, helpful atmosphere that you will love!

~Laurie Bonin

Company Chicken

Ingredients:
- 4 boneless skinless chicken breasts (about 1 pound) pounded
- 8-10 ounces fresh mushrooms, sliced
- 4 slices Muenster cheese to cover chicken
- 2 tablespoons butter
- 2 tablespoons oil
- ⅔ cup water
- 1 envelope chicken bouillon
- 2 tablespoons Wondra flour (plus enough to flour chicken)
- ⅓ cup white wine

Steps:
- Flour chicken
- Melt butter and oil in large skillet over medium high heat
- Brown breasts
- Remove to baking dish
- Cover with cheese slices
- Sauté mushrooms in skillet until slightly softened (add more butter and oil if needed)
- Put mushrooms over chicken
- Add water, bouillon and 2 tablespoons flour to skillet
- Stir until mixed
- Add ⅓ cup wine, mix and pour over chicken and cheese
- Cover with foil. If baking later, refrigerate
- Bake for 20 minutes at 350°
- Remove foil
- Bake an additional 10 minutes

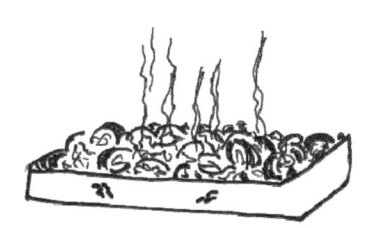

Serves 4

An easy recipe that can be prepared ahead and baked later. Can easily be doubled
~Eileen Gibb

Meats & Poultry

Mayo House

As you walk down Main Street, you will notice an antique three-quarter Cape house numbered 540. It was built by Josiah Mayo between 1818 and 1820. He married Desire Harding and they raised four children in this house. Josiah was postmaster for 40 years, town treasurer for 26 years, a blacksmith, ran a dry goods store and served a term as selectman.

In addition to housing Josiah's family, sections of the house served as a post office and dry goods store. The house was moved to its current location after the Cape Cod Five Cents Savings Bank bought it and then donated the house to the Chatham Conservation Foundation in 1976. The house is open for tours by docents during the summer and on special event weekends.

~Mary Ann Chamberlain

Railroad Museum

When I first moved to Chatham, my young grandson came for a visit. I took him to the playground and then noticed the caboose and railroad museum across the street. He loved playing in the caboose and looking at the dioramas inside the museum. This wonderful educational institution in our community provides a working model of a bygone era.

The museum is housed in a building that was the working train station in Chatham. It was founded in 1960 following the donation of the building and land. Frank Love, a retired New York Central Railroad executive, was the first director. He wrote to 62 railroad presidents seeking memorabilia. They generously donated many items. The museum now contains a Western Union telegraph, lanterns, badges, timetables, signs, passes and a 600-volume library. A diorama of the train system is the centerpiece and interesting to adults as well as children. Behind the museum is a restored 1910 wood sided caboose that includes sound effects of a moving train.

~Mary Ann Chamberlain

Chicken Chow Mein

Ingredients:
- oil
- 2 cups chopped onions
- 1½ cups chopped celery
- 8 ounce chopped mushrooms
- ¾ pound asparagus, cut in pieces
- 1 can sliced water chestnuts, drained
- 1 can low sodium chicken broth
- 2 teaspoons soy sauce
- 1 tablespoon corn starch
- 1 tablespoon water
- 1 pound cooked chicken, cut up

Steps:
- Put oil in pan, sauté onions and celery about 5 minutes
- Add mushrooms and asparagus, cover and cook about 10 minutes
- Add broth, chicken, other vegetables and soy sauce. Cook about 5 minutes
- Add mixture of cornstarch and water and cook until thickened
- Serve over rice

Add something crunchy, such as chow mein noodles, toasted almonds or cashews
The children love it with a side of egg rolls.

This meal serves at least 6 and you can change vegetables or add beef rather than chicken.

~Nancy Black

Labyrinth

In honor of the Chatham 300th Celebration, the Chatham Clergy Association and many other community supporters gifted a labyrinth to the town of Chatham in the spring of 2012. It is located at the end of Chase Park behind the Grist Mill. A labyrinth is not a maze. It is a one way in, one way out, circular path that can be used for meditation. Some use it as a kind of inner pilgrimage walk. It is meant to be a place of quiet reflection for anyone at any time. You may choose to walk it or even just sit on the specially made benches. It may be a special place for quiet and peace when troubles come upon you.

~Gail Smith

ASIAN ORANGE CHICKEN

Ingredients:
- 1 (3½ pound) chicken, cut up
- Salt and pepper to taste
- 1 (12 ounce) can frozen orange juice concentrate, thawed
- ¼ cup dry sherry
- ¼ cup Dijon mustard
- 3 tablespoons soy sauce
- 2 tablespoons peeled, minced ginger
- 4 garlic cloves, minced
- 4 scallions, thinly sliced (white and light green parts)
- Orange slices

Steps:
- Rinse chicken and pat dry; season with salt and pepper
- Place in a single layer in a shallow 9x13 inch glass baking dish
- Combine juice, sherry, mustard, soy sauce, ginger and garlic in a medium bowl and whisk together with a fork
- Pour all but ½ cup of the marinade over the chicken.
- Cover with plastic wrap and refrigerate at least 4 hours. Also refrigerate reserved marinade
- Preheat oven to 375°
- Take chicken out of marinade, shaking off excess and lightly patting with a paper towel
- Line a rimmed baking sheet with foil and then grease
- Place chicken in a single layer on the sheet
- Bake 1 hour, basting occasionally with reserved marinade
- Remove from oven and place cooked chicken on a platter
- Cool slightly, then cover with foil and refrigerate
- Serve cold garnished with scallions and orange slices

Serves: 4

Note: An alternate chicken choice would be to use 1 pound chicken drumsticks, 1 pound chicken thighs and 1 pound chicken wings, bone-in

An easy recipe to do. A summer treat which is good year round.
~Susan Turner Pinzuti

Meats & Poultry 87

Chicken Stew

Ingredients:
- 1 (3–4 pound) chicken
- 8 cups chicken stock
- Salt and pepper to taste
- 5 carrots, thickly sliced
- 4 medium leeks, thickly sliced
- 4 stalks celery, thickly sliced
- 4 cloves garlic, smashed
- ½ teaspoon dried thyme
- 1 bay leaf
- 4 sprigs flat leaf parsley
- ½ cup small pasta or orzo
- 3 tablespoons unsalted butter
- 1 tablespoon lemon juice
- 1 teaspoon dried tarragon
- ¼ cup flat leaf parsley, chopped
- 6 slices Italian (or firm crusted) bread
- ¼ cup extra virgin olive oil
- ½ cup grated Parmesan cheese

Steps:
- Place chicken in 6 quart pot, breast side down.
- Add stock, seasoned with salt and pepper. Bring to a boil
- Add the carrots, leeks, celery, garlic, thyme, bay leaf and springs of parsley and simmer
- After 15 minutes, flip the chicken and cook for 25 minutes more or until cooked thoroughly
- Remove the chicken and let cool
- Drain the vegetables, discarding the bay leaf and parsley. Return the stock to the pot and cook until reduced by half
- Remove meat from the chicken
- Add the pasta to the stock and cook for 3 – 4 minutes, then whisk in the butter, lemon juice, tarragon and parsley
- Add the chicken and vegetables and heat through

To serve: Place a piece of toasted bread in a bowl, drizzle with olive oil and sprinkle generously with Parmesan cheese and top with stew

Serves 6

This is definitely comfort food and delicious. Great for a chilly night's dinner along with a salad and warm bread.
~Susan Adsit

Enriching Our Communities

The Women's Club of Chatham (WCC) supports our communities by organizing fundraisers to provide scholarships and grants for worthy recipients and local organizations and through individual contributions from our members for local families.

We donate to the Cape Cod Community College Education Foundation's "On Their Way Program." This scholarship is designed to assist the non-traditional student who is returning or has returned to college after an interruption and has a financial need. The WCC establishes the criteria which is used by the Foundation to choose the recipients.

The grants are offered to organizations or groups that have a presence in Chatham and Harwich and seek funding for a specific project or need. Grants recently funded included a computer for the Community Center and an iPad at the Eldredge Public Library for teaching patrons how to download books. The grant applications are available from the WCC from January through February. All grants are thoughtfully reviewed and awards are made in April after approval from the Board.

Many of the Women's Club projects center on families. One of our favorites is "Adopt-a-Child" at Christmas time. We provide presents for the children of approximately ten families. Club members generously purchase clothes, toys and gift cards. We also have food drives to help stock the shelves of the local food pantries.

For an organization called Cape Cod Cares for the Troops, club members donate money and personal care items and extend holiday wishes on signed personalized holiday cards.

~Ann Wade/Robin Zibrat

Quick Chicken Curry

Ingredients:
- 1½ tablespoons olive oil
- 1 small onion, thinly sliced
- 2 teaspoons curry powder
- ½ cup plain yogurt
- ¾ cup heavy cream
- ½ teaspoon kosher salt
- ¼ teaspoon black pepper
- 1 (14½ ounce) can diced tomatoes, drained (optional)
- 1 rotisserie chicken
- 2 cup cooked white rice
- ¼ cup fresh cilantro leaves, roughly chopped

Steps:
- Heat oil in a large skillet over medium-low heat
- Add onion and cook, stirring occasionally for 7 minutes
- Sprinkle with the curry powder and cook stirring for 1 minute
- Add yogurt and cream and simmer gently for 3 minutes
- Stir in the salt, pepper and tomatoes (if using)
- Remove from heat
- Slice or shred the chicken, discarding the skin and bones
- Place the rice and chicken on a platter and spoon sauce over the top
- Sprinkle with cilantro

Serves 4 – 6

~Rose Marie McLoughlin

Serving Our Town

To serve our town is a privilege. It is satisfying for the members of Chatham's Finance Committee to join with Town Meeting members each spring to set the course that our town will take in future years. The nine of us are appointed by the Town Moderator based on our varied life experience. We study proposals from town officials on how the town budget is to be apportioned. We comment at the Town Meeting on the financial prudence of these budget proposals. We feel privileged to help in shaping the face that Chatham turns to the world today and in the years to come.

~Jo Ann Sprague

HOT CHICKEN SALAD

Ingredients:
- 2 pounds cooked chicken breast meat, cubed
- 1 cup celery, diced
- 1 cup slivered almonds
- ½ teaspoon salt
- ½ teaspoon pepper
- 1 cup mayonnaise
- 1 cup shredded white sharp cheddar cheese
- 1 cup crushed potato chips – kettle cooked chips work the best

Steps:
- Preheat oven to 350°
- Spray a 9 x 13 inch baking dish
- Combine the first 7 ingredients in large mixing bowl
- Put in baking dish
- Spread potato chips on top
- Bake for 25-30 minutes or until bubbling

Serves 10-12

Perfect for a potluck supper in the cooler months.
~Eileen Gibb

The League of Women Voters

The skirts were long -- warm in the winter and hot in the summer -- when the League of Women Voters (the League or LWV) formed as an organization after women got the right to vote in 1920. That same year the League came to Massachusetts. Four decades later, when skirts had shortened considerably, this non-partisan political organization came to the Cape.

Cape-wide the LWV of the Cape Cod Area provides voter education and voter service and sponsors educational programs of regional importance on such subjects as wastewater and mental health. It co-sponsors candidate meetings for members of the state legislature and, when requested, provides moderators for town elections.

Did you ever notice those yellow and red signs at Town Meeting that help speakers and the moderator know when the time limit is up for speaking? They are held up by League volunteers with stopwatches. In our town of Chatham, the League sponsors a candidates forum each spring to help voters differentiate between the candidates. In addition, it often invites the town manager to review the Annual Town Meeting Warrant with members and their guests. The League remains as it has always been -- a group of thoughtful citizens, committed to making democracy effective and vital. League membership is open to both men and women who believe that democracy is not a "spectator sport."

~Judy Thomas

Social Clubs

We showed up at our first Newcomers' meeting a few months after we retired to our Chatham home. There were gorgeous beaches here, a friendly bar and grill, but nothing social happened. After this meeting, the power of social contact filled this void by connecting us to people and activities.

We were members of Newcomers for five years and then joined another social club, CONCH Cape Cod, where we continued to make more connections and to live more active lives. With new Chatham friends we partied, hiked, learned to invest in stock, dined around, went out to breakfast and travelled both abroad and throughout the United States. We formed a marching band and blew conch shells in the July 4th parade celebrating Chatham's 300 years. We volunteered to lead and organize various activities and through that commitment, found friendship and fulfillment.

Friends encouraged me to join The Women's Club of Chatham and it is there I found a place to enjoy the company of women, eat tea sandwiches and enrich the community. My husband later joined the Chatham Retired Men's Association and there he found a place to enjoy men's jokes, eat donuts and observe a schedule of interesting weekly speakers. Social clubs gave us the gift of belonging. Life is good.

~Regina McDowell

EASY, ELEGANT TURKEY & SPINACH

Ingredients:
- 1 pound ground turkey (or ground beef)
- ½ small onion, finely chopped
- ½ package mushrooms, finely chopped
- 2 tablespoons butter (or butter and olive oil, 1 tablespoon each)
- 1 clove pressed garlic
- 2-3 cups fresh spinach, washed and chopped
- 1 egg
- ½ cup bread crumbs
- ½ cup dry red wine
- Salt, pepper, fresh parsley

Steps:
- Sauté onion and mushrooms in butter (or butter and oil) in large frying pan until lightly browned
- Add garlic and spinach and mix until spinach wilts
- Remove from heat
- Beat egg in a large bowl
- Add ground turkey, bread crumbs, onion / mushroom/spinach mixture and 2 tablespoons red wine
- Mix gently
- Season with salt and pepper
- Shape into 4 large or 6 small patties
- Reheat frying pan, add butter and/or oil and brown patties over med high heat about 4 minutes per side
- Remove patties to warm platter, keep warm
- Pour remaining 6 tablespoons red wine to pan
- Cook, stirring to mix in pan drippings
- Boil for about 30 seconds
- Pour over patties, sprinkle with chopped parsley

This is a quick, easy and healthy weeknight dinner for the family but tasty enough for company too.

~Cece Motz

Newcomers

Retirement! For most of us who now reside in Chatham and Harwich, it meant leaving friends and daily activities to live fulltime in a different location. How will I meet new friends? What activities will I find and who will I do them with?

Luckily, 35 years ago a group of people started an organization to bring new residents together and develop activities they could share. That group is now called Chatham-Harwich Newcomers. It is much more than your average Newcomers Club as we are almost 500 members strong. It provides a true community gathering platform for about 25 different activities and social events: hiking, bowling, fine dining, men's cooking, woodworking, kayaking, book clubs, knitting and women's gourmet to name a few. It has become a dynamic and integral part of many of our lives and, if you ever move to Chatham, it's one of the first things to check out.

~Alice Reed

STUFFED CABBAGE

Ingredients:
- ¾ cup rice
- 2 cups water
- Medium head of green cabbage
- 1-1½ pound meatloaf mix
  (beef, veal and pork)
- Salt and pepper
- 1 small onion
- 2 tablespoons butter or margarine
- 1 egg
- Can of tomato soup

Steps:
- Cook the rice in about 2 cups water until water evaporates. Cool
- Sauté onion in 2 tablespoons butter/margarine and set aside
- Core cabbage and put in a pot of boiling water until leaves are soft
- Remove leaves and cool

Stuffing:
- In a bowl add beef/pork, salt and pepper to taste, onion and egg. Mix together
- Add cooked rice and be sure to mix well

Assemble:
- Place about 1 tablespoon of stuffing mixture in each cabbage leaf and wrap
- Place in a large pot and add a can of tomato soup with just enough water to cover the stuffed cabbage
- Sprinkle with just a little salt and pepper
- Cover and cook on low heat for 1-1½ hours

This dish has become a traditional favorite in my family. It was passed down from my grandmother to me. We all consider it to be our family's comfort food.
~Lorraine Cocolis

Golfer's Stew

Ingredients:
- 1½ pounds stew beef cut into 1 inch pieces
- 3 medium onions, sliced
- 1 (14 ounce) can tomatoes, chopped
- 1 cup celery, cut into 1 inch pieces
- 3 or 4 carrots, cut into 1 inch pieces
- 2 teaspoons salt
- 3 tablespoons tapioca
- 1 (8 ounce) can tomato sauce

Steps:
- Mix all ingredients together
- Bake in covered casserole 5 hours at 250° or cook in your slow cooker

Serves 4 to 6

This is easy to assemble and is ready when you come home tired.
~Alice Reed

Trash to Treasure

When we came to Chatham in the 60s, we stayed in a home on Sam Ryder Road. Some of our favorite outings were going to the Band Concerts on Friday nights, swimming at Schoolhouse Pond and going to the town dump, now known as the Transfer Station. There was never a paved road but several dirt ones that led to different parts of the dump: one for appliances, one for rubbish and others for clothing and furniture. It was here that we learned from my grandparents about antiques.

On one trip we found a solid oak kitchen table and four matching chairs with lovely decals on the backs, but unfortunately the wicker seats were broken. Instead of weaving the wicker we simply replaced the seats with a patterned fiber board, repainted and used them for several years. Chairs were often updated to replace the ones we had brought back from previous trips and I was told about their style and why one was better than another. Other "finds" were a gate leg table which replaced a side table because it was smaller and an oak tea cart for a plant stand. Even the gas stove was replaced by a newer model which had four burners and a larger oven with a family of mice living inside.

I still own several antiques and my brother went into the antique business. Two of my children now appreciate good solid wooden furniture and one loves to go "Dumpster Diving" looking for a treasure. What fun it has been to become good "pickers" and to create treasures from trash.

~Marilyn Sink

Community Garden

There is magic in any garden and that magic is magnified in the Community Garden. Twenty six 20' x 20' plots keep more than forty gardeners busy from May to November. The garden is located on Route 28 at Old Queen Anne Road.

The idea for a community garden was born in the produce section of a local supermarket when Florence Seldin and Mary Ellen Sussman expressed a desire for people to be able to grow instead of buy veggies. Mary Ellen and I carried on with a lot of help from town businesses and organizations. Generous donations of time, money and expertise were given in planning and building a garden from a vacant weed-filled lot. A list of our many donors can be seen on the shed in the garden. We had our first season in 2011 and since then have produced many pounds of vegetables for our own and others' consumption.

The garden in August is a sight to behold. Neat paths frame gardens bursting with vegetables, herbs and flowers. Bees buzz, birds sing and the gardeners harvest the fruits of their labors.

~Heidi Quill

BRISKET & BEANS

Ingredients:
- 4 pounds first cut brisket
- 1 can tomato soup
- 1 can hot water
- 1 teaspoon baking soda
- 6 tablespoons dark brown sugar
- 6 tablespoons dark molasses
- 1 medium onion sliced
- 1 tablespoon paprika
- 2 cups large lima beans (soak overnight in water and drain prior to using)

Steps:
- Brown brisket in a large pot.
- Remove brisket and wipe out pot
- Place ½ of sliced onion in pot and add brisket
- Sprinkle both sides of meat with paprika
- Combine baking soda, mustard, 3 tablespoons brown sugar and 3 tablespoons molasses until light brown and smooth
- Add lima beans to molasses mixture and stir to coat
- Add remaining onion to mixture
- Pour mixture over and around beef
- In the bowl used to mix beans add tomato soup and water. Mix well
- Pour over beans and beef

Bake for 4 hours at 350°
- After 2½ hours of baking, slice beef diagonally
- While meat is out of pot, add 3 tablespoons brown sugar and 3 tablespoons molasses and stir well
- Return meat to pot
- Push down so liquid covers meat
- Bake the remaining 1½ hours

~Rose Marie McLoughlin

Council on Aging

You might be active, involved in your own activities, busy with family and friends, but the day might come when you are here in Chatham and your life style has changed. The Council on Aging (COA), a town department designated to serve the needs of seniors, might be something you will want to check into. In fact, if you are 60 years or older, you might enjoy many of its activities now.

Lunches on Mondays are gourmet status and a first or second run movie is shown once a month. The computer school, available to all regardless of age, will keep you up to speed in the newest equipment. Many enjoy Scrabble and cribbage. A quick check on your blood pressure, help with your toenails, a massage or a hearing test are all provided by trained professionals. What a wonderful way to get a quick check to help keep you young. Should you need a wheelchair, walker or cane for a short time, there might be one there for you or your houseguest to borrow.

~Betsey Stevens

The First Congregational Church of Chatham

The First Congregational Church of Chatham traces its origin to 1665 when William Nickerson brought his family to Monomoit, as the area was then known. The Plymouth Colony Court, in 1679, ordered the inhabitants of the area "to raise among themselves five pounds a year in money and other substantial goods" for the purpose of building a meeting house, a prerequisite for incorporating a town. In 1697 Jonathan Vickery, who was paid in hay, became the first minister. In the early years a minister might have been expected to serve as preacher, pastor, doctor, surgeon, lawyer and/or judge. A new and enlarged building served as the church until the present church was built in 1830 on a site known as Union Cemetery. It was later moved to its present location on Main Street.

The chandelier in the sanctuary has hung there since 1848. Lightning struck the church steeple in 1887. The steeple was such an important landmark for ships at sea that it was promptly repaired. The ornament at the top came from the barque, R. A. Allen, which was wrecked on the Monomoy shoals.

Today The First Congregational Church of Chatham is a bustle of activity. Each summer art shows and tie dyeing take place on the front lawn. In the fall, hundreds of pumpkins grace the lawn to raise funds for the Children's Fund of the Chatham teachers. In December a community chorus presents a Christmas concert and, on First Night, a lasagna dinner is served while the church is open for musical events.

~Doris Philips

LONDON BROIL

Ingredients:
- 1 (2-2½ pounds) flank steak
- 2 teaspoons unseasoned meat tenderizer
- 1 tablespoon sugar
- 2 tablespoons dry sherry
- 2 tablespoons soy sauce
- 1 tablespoon honey
- 1 teaspoon salt
- 1 teaspoon Accent seasoning

Steps:
- Pierce surface of steak at one inch intervals with sharp fork
- Combine remaining ingredients and pour over steak
- Marinate about one hour, turning occasionally
- Broil or grill, allowing 3 to 5 minutes each side
- To serve, cut thin slices against the grain

Serves 6-8

An easy and tasty dish for all seasons since it can be done on the grill or in the broiler. Be sure to use unseasoned meat tenderizer.
~Laurie Bonin

The Chatham Chorale

The Chatham Chorale was founded in 1970 by Marjorie (Jerry) Bennett Morley and Dr. E. Robert Harned. The original singers were from the Congregational churches in Harwich and Chatham. Olive Cahoon was the first accompanist. The group now has over 100 singers who come from all parts of Cape Cod. In 1977 a smaller select ensemble, the Chatham Chorale Chamber Singers, was established. Jerry Morley directed the chorale for seventeen years. Upon her retirement in 1987, Margaret Bossi became the group's director, leading the ensemble for the next 23 years. Joseph Marchio, appointed Music Director in 2010, now leads the Chatham Chorale. Donald Enos has been the accompanist since 1986.

The Chorale and the Chamber Singers give five to six sets of concerts each year. The programs range from the most challenging classical works to lighter music such as the recent very popular Celtic concerts. The Chatham Chorale performs regularly with the Cape Cod Symphony Orchestra at their Holiday Pops concerts and in their major works such as Guiseppe Verdi's Requiem and the Resurrection Symphony by Gustav Mahler.

~Doris Philips

BONELESS ROAST PORK WITH PLUM SAUCE

Ingredients:
- 1 (3 pound) boneless pork loin roast
- 2 cloves garlic minced
- 1 teaspoon ground sage
- ½ teaspoon black pepper

Plum Sauce Ingredients:
- ½ cup plum jam
- 1½ tablespoons red wine vinegar
- 1 tablespoon soy sauce
- ½ teaspoon dry mustard
- ⅛ teaspoon ground allspice

Steps:
- Combine garlic, sage and pepper
- Rub mix over entire roast
- Place on rack in roasting pan
- Insert meat thermometer into thickest part
- Bake uncovered at 325° for about 2 hours or until 170° is reached

Plum Sauce Steps:
- Combine all ingredients in small sauce pan
- Bring to boil
- Reduce heat and cook 2 minutes, stirring constantly
- Spread a portion of the sauce over roast during the last half hour of cooking
- Serve the remainder of the sauce at the table

Note: Sauce may be doubled

Serves 6 – 8

A fine entrée for family or guest. We love it.
~Edie Ward

Second Homes

I never tire of listening to second homeowners as they describe their love for Chatham and its natural beauty. Their comments always seem to follow a common thread as they talk about the long walks on Lighthouse or Hardings Beach, the sighting of seals around Monomoy, the calm of the children's beach at Oyster Pond, band concerts, the Fourth of July parade and always the small town feel that Chatham has maintained.

They say that it is the physical attraction that brought them to Chatham's unique natural environment that doesn't exist elsewhere. With miles of National Seashore and wildlife refuges, Chatham is surrounded on three sides by Nantucket Sound, Pleasant Bay and the Atlantic Ocean. These homeowners were drawn here because Chatham is somewhat off the beaten path and a true destination lying 35 miles into the ocean and often experiences its own weather.

Another aspect that keeps second homeowners and the washashores here is Chatham's deep tradition of welcoming strangers. Chatham attracts an enormous variety of people because they are made to feel welcome. They add a wonderful diversity to the working community of fishermen, homebuilders, craftsmen and all the others who have a love for the ocean and marine and wildlife. Second homeowners enjoy knowing that Chatham is a mecca for migrating birds and waterfowl, as they stop in Chatham along the migratory route from the Arctic to South America and back. These homeowners come from all across the United States and many countries throughout the world. They constitute 60 percent of the residents in Chatham. Many will eventually move permanently to Chatham in their retirement, choosing a kinder and gentler life style and the opportunity to thrive in a beautiful coastal environment. What a delightful thought! Can you blame them?

~Ella Leavitt

VEAL MILANESE
~ ARUGULA, TOMATO & RED ONION SALAD ~

Veal Ingredients:
- 1 cup flour
- Salt and black pepper
- 2 eggs
- 2 tablespoons water
- 1 cup finely ground bread crumbs (preferably panko)
- 1 pinch fresh thyme leaves, chopped
- 1 pinch fresh rosemary, chopped
- 2 (5 ounce) pieces boneless veal loin, pounded very thin, about ¼ inch thick
- 4 ounces (½ cup) extra-virgin olive oil

Steps:
- Place the flour in a shallow pan and season with salt and pepper.
- Lightly beat the eggs and water in another shallow pan and season with salt and pepper.
- Combine the breads crumbs, thyme and rosemary in a third shallow pan and season with salt and pepper.
- Arrange the flour, egg wash and bread crumb pans in a line in front of you and have a clean platter or pan ready to hold the dredged veal
- Working with one piece at a time, season the veal with salt and pepper
- Dip the cutlet in the flour, shaking off any excess, then in the egg wash, allowing the excess egg to drain back into the pan
- Finally, dip the cutlet in the bread crumbs, pressing gently to coat evenly, and place on the clean platter or pan
- Refrigerate for at least one hour, or up to six hours
- Heat the olive oil in a large skillet over high heat.
- When the oil is hot, add the veal and cook about 3 minutes per side, shaking the pan back and forth every 30 seconds or so to create a crisp, golden brown crust
- Transfer the veal to a plate lined with several layers of paper towels to soak up any excess oil and season with salt and pepper

Salad Ingredients:
- 1 large bunch arugula, rinsed and dried
- 1 bunch frisée, rinsed and dried (if you cannot find frisée, double the amount of arugula)
- 1 ripe plum tomato, diced into small pieces
- ½ red onion, thinly sliced
- 2 ounces (¼ cup) extra-virgin olive oil
- Juice of 1 lemon
- Salt and pepper, to taste

Steps for the Salad:
- Combine the arugula, frisée, tomato and onion in a mixing bowl
- Toss the salad with the olive oil, the juice of half the lemon, salt and pepper

To Serve
- Place the veal in the center of two plates, top with the salad, drizzle the remaining lemon juice and serve

Makes 2 lunch or dinner portions

This recipe also works well with chicken breast or loin of pork.

~Ella Leavitt

Historic Buildings on Main Street

On Main Street, from The First Congregational Church to the Isaac Hardy home near School Street, there are 18 historic structures that make a lovely historical walk through time. The reference librarian at Eldredge Public Library put together a walking map for the tercentennial celebration in Chatham.

The structures vary. Included on the map are homes, stores, public buildings and churches. There is even a former stable and blacksmith shop which now houses Yankee Ingenuity. The building where you find Canterbury Leather started out as a grain store in the 400 block of Main Street. This building was moved to land near the Mayo House where it became a hardware and tin shop. It was then moved to its present location and ultimately became Chatham's first A & P Market. When the market moved across the street to what is now Ben Franklin, the shop became an artist studio. Even the St. Christopher's Episcopal Church building started out as the meeting hall for the Universalist Community which later moved to the Christian Science building when that congregation relocated to Harwich.

And so it goes. Every building has a story and anyone with a good imagination can look back through time and wonder how they would have fit into this picture of an ever-evolving physical landscape.

~Sharon Oudemool

COMPETITIONS

Eastward Ho! View *Painting by Judith Kelley*

Casseroles & Vegetables

Eastward Ho!

A seaside gem, awesome views, exciting, challenging - these are but a few of the superlatives describing this private links golf club. The design was entrusted to W. Herbert Fowler of London, England. It opened for play on July 3, 1922 with an exhibition featuring Francis Ouimet. The course is surrounded by Pleasant Bay on three sides with striking views of the barrier beach and the Atlantic Ocean beyond. It offers some of the most dramatic golfing terrain and vistas on the East Coast.

Eastward Ho! is proud of the support it gives the community. The annual Cape Cod Hospital Benefit, with two golf tournaments and a festive evening, raises remarkable financial support. Twice a year on daylight change dates the golf course is opened without charge to Chatham residents. Reward yourself. Take a drive on Fox Hill Road and feast your eyes on the fabulous views of this challenging links course.

~Edie Ward

Cucumbers with Vinegar, Oil & Parsley

Ingredients:
- 2-3 cucumbers, thinly sliced
- 1 teaspoon sea salt
- 1 teaspoon sugar
- 1 teaspoon white vinegar
- 1 small onion

Dressing Ingredients
- ¼ cup white vinegar
- ½ cup water
- 1 tablespoon canola oil
- Parsley (to taste)

Steps:
- Place the first five ingredients in a bowl
- Let mixture set for several hours or overnight. Drain
- Rinse well in cold water
- After cucumbers are drained, mix the dressing ingredients
- Pour over cucumbers. Mix well
- Best when chilled

This recipe was handed down to me by my mother. It is particularly good in the summer when cucumbers are just picked from the garden.

~Lorraine Cocolis

Pleasant Bay Community Boating

Have you driven by Pleasant Bay in the summer and seen gaggles of kids rollicking and sailing near a narrow sand beach below Eastward Ho!? They are sailing with Pleasant Bay Community Boating (PBCB). Now in its 11th year, PBCB's goal is to make sailing on Cape Cod's Pleasant Bay affordable and accessible to everyone, to "sailors without boats."

PBCB provides free instruction to the Monomoy Community Services program participants and Special Olympics sailors. It also hosts the Cumming Cup U.S. Sailing event and the Friends of Pleasant Bay Regatta. PBCB provides sailing lessons to those between ages 8 and 17 as well as adults and rents its boats on weekends to members who know how to sail. From grandchildren to grandparents, the key words are SAILING FUN. Come learn to skipper a sailboat and enjoy Pleasant Bay!

~Eve Dalmolen

Casseroles & Vegetables

Chatham Walkers

If you've seen a group of people walking through Chatham in the morning and thought it was a neat idea and you should join them, you were noticing the Chatham Walkers. This group has been walking since 1985 - three miles on Tuesday, Thursday and Saturday mornings year round. Most of those days they start from Oyster Pond at 7:00 a.m. -- 7:30 a.m. in the winter. Sometimes the month's volunteer leader selects a different route, such as a bike path in Orleans, or a conservation area in Harwich or even a park in Wellfleet.

The group has as little structure as possible. There are no dues, no attendance and no requirements. Ages seem to range from 50 up, but every once in a while grandchildren will join the group to see if they can outwalk their grandparents.

Walking, we all know, is good for us. It keeps the legs strong, helps the breathing and burns the calories. The companionship found in walking with a group is also a great benefit. Participants walk the three miles (or as much as they wish) at their own speed and there is always someone else moving at that same rate. New walkers are always welcome.

~Betsey Stevens

Cheddar & Sausage Breakfast Casserole

Ingredients:
- 1 pound ground pork sausage
- 10 slices of white bread, cubed to make 6 cups
- 2 cups sharp cheddar cheese, shredded
- 6 large eggs
- 2 cups milk
- 1 teaspoon dry mustard
- ¼ to ½ teaspoon Worcestershire sauce

Steps:
- Cook sausage over medium heat until no longer pink; drain well
- Place bread cubes in lightly greased 13 x 9 inch dish
- Sprinkle cheese over bread and top with sausage
- Whisk together eggs and rest of ingredients
- Pour evenly over sausage mixture
- Cover and chill for at least 8 hours
- Let stand at room temperature for 30 minutes
- Bake at 350° for 45 minutes or until set
- Take out and let stand for 5 minutes before serving

My sister and I had a wedding brunch shower for our niece and this breakfast item was enjoyed by all. We also serve it at our annual breakfast for the Chatham Walkers.

~Sue Simpson

Turkey Trot

Wild turkeys aren't the only ones who get to trot around Chatham on Thanksgiving morning! Adult human participants, after a donation of fifteen dollars and a bag full of groceries for the Family Pantry, get their turn running or walking the Chatham loop. Many children 15 and under participate for $5, some in strollers, and a few well behaved dogs join the parade. To date, thousands of people have participated and raised many thousands of dollars for the Lower Cape Outreach Council. Participants receive cleverly designed t-shirts to commemorate a wonderful way to start Thanksgiving Day.

~Joyce Sterling

Reuben Bake

Ingredients:
- 1 (8 ounce) package noodles, cooked and drained
- 4 tablespoons melted butter
- 1 pound sauerkraut, slightly drained
- ¾-1 pound corned beef, thinly sliced
- 1 cup Russian dressing
- 2 cups Swiss cheese, shredded
- ½ teaspoon caraway seed
- ⅛ teaspoon garlic powder
- 1 cup or more rye crackers, crushed
- 3-4 tomatoes, thinly sliced

Steps:
- Preheat oven to 350°
- Mix noodles with 2 tablespoons melted butter
- Place in bottom of 9x13 inch pan
- Toss sauerkraut with caraway seeds and garlic powder
- Top noodles with sauerkraut and sliced corned beef
- Spread Russian dressing on top and add tomato slices
- Cover with shredded Swiss cheese
- Mix crackers with remaining 2 tablespoons butter as final layer
- Bake 35 minutes or until hot and bubbly
- Let stand for 20 minutes before serving

Note: Rye crackers are important!

A good buffet or potluck dish.
~Susan Turner Pinzuti

April Fools' Plunge

From what started as a spur of the moment tribute to a family member of a Chatham firefighter, a community fundraiser tradition was born. On April 1, 2008, ten Chatham firefighters decided that when their shift was over, they would take to the brisk Chatham waters for a dip as a way to honor the memory of a family member who had recently passed away from cancer and who had traditionally participated in an April Fools' Day Polar Bear plunge.

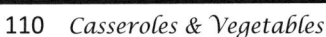

Chicken & Noodle Supreme

Ingredients:
- 2 pounds chicken, cubed
- ¼ cup flour
- 2 teaspoon salt
- ¼ teaspoon pepper
- 4 tablespoons butter
- ½ onion, sliced
- 1 cup water
- 1 (6 ounce) package noodles
- 1 cup mushrooms, sliced
- 1 teaspoons celery seed
- 1 cup sour cream
- ½ cup bread crumbs, buttered

Steps:
- Roll chicken in flour, dust off excess. Brown in butter
- Add onions and water. Simmer until tender about 1–1½ hours
- Cook noodles until almost tender. Drain
- Add chicken mixture, mushrooms, celery seed and sour cream to noodles
- Season with salt and pepper to taste
- Turn into a buttered 1½ quart casserole
- Top with buttered crumbs
- Bake at 300° for 45 minutes

My mother began making this casserole in the 1940s. The recipe is especially suited for large buffets.
~Liz Schmid Hines

Little did these firemen know they were spearheading what is now a long-standing tradition in Chatham. Each year on this day, come rain or shine, warm temperatures or not, Chatham's Fire Department sponsors The Plunge followed by a free barbequed dinner as a fundraising event to benefit a local family who is suffering from illness or injury. Over these past years hundreds of Chatham area residents and visitors have taken to our chilly waters as a fun way to celebrate April Fools' Day while knowing they are directly helping a neighbor in need. Even our neighboring towns of Brewster and Harwich contribute the use of their hook and ladder engines for hoisting an American flag to celebrate the event.
~Jennifer Reed

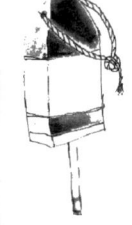

PILGRIM POTATOES

Ingredients:
- 5 pounds Yukon Gold potatoes (about 9 large)
- 6 ounces cream cheese, softened
- 1 cup sour cream
- 1 teaspoon onion salt
- ½ teaspoon pepper
- ⅓ stick butter
- ¾ cup milk

Steps:
- Peel potatoes and cook in boiling water until tender, about 20 minutes
- Drain and mash until smooth. When smooth continue to beat, gradually add remaining ingredients
- Beat until light and fluffy
- Put in 2 quart casserole
- Dot with butter and cover

Note: This dish can be made and stored in the refrigerator several days before serving. To heat, bake in 350° oven for about 40 minutes

Makes 10 to 12 servings

This is a wonderful dish to prepare a day or two before Thanksgiving to avoid same day stress. It is delicious.

~Joanne Donoghue

POTATOES ROMANOFF

Ingredients:
- 8 large potatoes
- 2 (10 ounce each) sour cream
- 1 bunch green onions, chopped
- 1¾ cup shredded sharp cheddar cheese
- 2 teaspoons salt
- ¼ teaspoon pepper
- Paprika

Steps:
- Cook potatoes in the jackets till tender, then peel
- Shred potatoes into a large bowl
- Stir in sour cream, 1 cup cheddar cheese, onions, salt and pepper
- Turn mixture into a buttered 2-3 quart casserole baking dish
- Top with remaining cheddar cheese
- Sprinkle paprika on top of the mixture
- Refrigerate the mixture overnight
- Bake uncovered in preheated oven at 350° for 40 minutes

Serves 8-10

Delicious!
~Meg Cimini

Sweet Potatoes with Pecans & Bourbon

Ingredients:
- 6 pounds sweet potatoes
- 3 tablespoons bourbon
- 8 ounces unsalted butter
- Salt and pepper, to taste
- 2 cups pecan halves
- 1 teaspoon salt
- 2 tablespoons brown sugar

Steps:
- Prick sweet potatoes with a fork and bake until tender; approximately 1 hour at 425°
- When cool, peel potatoes and transfer half to a food processor
- Add bourbon and 6 tablespoons butter and puree 30 seconds; transfer to a large bowl
- Puree remaining potatoes until smooth; add to bowl
- Mix to combine
- Season with salt and pepper to taste and transfer to a 2-quart shallow oven-proof dish
- Spread pecans on a greased baking dish
- Bake at 325° degrees until fragrant, about 10 minutes
- Toss hot pecans with remaining 2 tablespoons butter and 1 teaspoon salt
- Arrange pecans on top of potatoes and sprinkle with brown sugar
- Bake at 350° until heated through

This can be made ahead and refrigerated before adding the pecans and baking to make a beautiful, yet simple, vegetable.

~Susan Adsit

SESAME SNOW PEAS

Ingredients:
- 3 tablespoons sesame oil
- 1 pound of snow peas
- 10 thin scallions, chopped
- 2 tablespoons pine nuts
- 1 tablespoon toasted sesame seeds
- Salt and pepper to taste

Steps:
- Heat oil. Add peas and scallions
- Sauté 3 minutes on medium heat
- Add nuts and seeds, salt and pepper
- Cook 2-3 minutes (do not overcook)

A delicious quick vegetable dish. Bon Appetit!
~Susan Turner Pinzuti

Stage Harbor Sailing School

Stage Harbor Yacht Club (SHYC), founded in 1932, is much more than a sailing club for adults. In 1937 they began offering sailing instruction, incorporating as Stage Harbor Sailing School in 1986, and now serve as many as 200 children each summer. Scholarships are given to local year-round residents. Unlike many sailing programs the Stage Harbor Sailing School owns its own fleet of boats, helping to keep instruction affordable. There are over 30 instructors from this country's most elite collegiate sailing programs who first learned to sail at SHYC.

Each summer young sailors from other clubs on the Cape come to Chatham for the Opti Regatta at Stage Harbor. They compete in one of four fleets according to age and skill level. It is absolutely amazing to see 100 small boats, which look like bathtubs with sails, sailing out of Stage Harbor.

~Martha Batchelder

BROCCOLI CHEESE CASSEROLE

Ingredients:
- 1 (16 ounce) package frozen broccoli florets
- 1 cup mayonnaise
- 1 teaspoon onion, chopped
- 1 cup grated Velveeta cheese
- ¾ cup mushroom soup
- 1 egg well beaten
- 1½ cup crushed Cheez-It crackers
- Salt & pepper to taste

Steps:
- Cook broccoli as directed on package and drain
- Combine remaining ingredients except Cheez-Its
- Mix well
- Stir in broccoli
- Pour into baking dish
- Sprinkle with Cheez-It crumbs
- Cook at 400° for 20 minutes

So quick and easy but so very yummy... even the next day!
~Jennifer Reed

House Hunting in Chatham

I attacked the internet each afternoon after work. I had the Chatham Chronicle sent. We spent lots of weekends traveling the four hours to check out houses. We struck up a relationship with our real estate agent. He looked for houses in our price range and location so we could walk to town—a must for us. Several years went by with no success and I got desperate. Reality set in concerning price and availability and then it happened.

Our agent called on Labor Day weekend and said to get to Chatham quickly. As we were speeding down the Mass Pike he was writing the contract, knowing when we saw the house we would say yes. We walked in through the kitchen and my husband took just one look and said, "OK, this one is the one." We finally had our Chatham home; then I began obsessing about how to furnish it.

~Susan Buoniconti

Geocaching

One of the best presents that I've ever given my techie husband is a hand-held GPS. With it, he discovered geocaching, a combination of technology and outdoor adventure. Our whole family now enjoys geocaching and we've discovered some amazing locations because of it. An online website specifies, using latitude and longitude, where geocaches are hidden. Using the GPS and clues in the description, you travel to the location, find the cache and sign the logbook. There are several dozen caches in Chatham, more than a thousand on the Cape and millions worldwide!

Some of the best geocaches we have found have been on Cape Cod. A geocache is often hidden in a place that the person hiding it wants to share. Thanks to geocaching, we've discovered hidden bays and beautiful vistas and hiked on beaches, in conservation areas and on new trails that we might never have found.

In turn, we've created several caches in Chatham that we have published on the geocaching website. That way, we can share some of our favorite places in Chatham with the geocaching community of over six million!

~Sue Simpson

CARROT PENNIES

Ingredients:
- 2 pounds sliced carrots
- 1 teaspoon salt
- 1 teaspoon pepper
- 1 cup chopped onions
- 1 cup chopped green pepper
- 1 can Campbell's tomato soup
- ¾ cup sugar
- ½ cup salad oil
- ½ cup vinegar
- 1 teaspoon Worcestershire sauce

Steps:
- Scrape carrots
- Cook whole, about 20 minutes
- Drain, cool
- Slice carrots
- Mix other ingredients
- Pour over carrots.

Note: This must be assembled at least one or two days ahead as it needs 24 hours to marinate. Keep refrigerated. Serve with slotted spoon or drain the marinade off first.

Serves 10-12

A do-ahead, these carrots always are a hit at dinner parties, tailgating and picnics. This is a good vegetable side dish.

~ Laurie Bonin

CARROT SOUFFLÉ

Ingredients:
- 1 pound carrots, peeled and cooked
- 3 eggs
- ⅓ cup granulated sugar
- 1 teaspoon baking powder
- ½ cup melted butter
- 2 tablespoons flour
- 1 teaspoon vanilla extract
- Dash of cinnamon
- Dash of nutmeg

Steps:
- Puree cooked carrots in a blender or food processor
- Add eggs to the carrots and puree
- Add sugar, flour, baking powder, vanilla, butter, cinnamon and nutmeg.
- Puree until smooth
- Pour into a 1½ quart casserole
- Bake for 1 hour at 350°

Note: Can be doubled for a large group, just have to do the processing in batches.

Serves 4 but more as it is usually a side to other dishes.

My niece, Mary Lee, always serves this on Thanksgiving. It is a nice addition to New England vegetables normally served with the turkey. I serve it at gatherings throughout the year and I like to take it if I'm asked to bring a side dish for a dinner party.

~Joanna Schurmann

Biking

Biking in Chatham is an experience not to be missed. When you bike the side streets and coastal roads of a town as beautiful as Chatham, you are able to appreciate all of its heritage -- natural, historic and cultural. Visitors who bike into Chatham often arrive via the Cape Cod Rail Trail from Harwich. This portion of the trail was connected in 2004 and is known as the Old Colony Trail and provides bikers with a safe and relaxed environment without the distraction of motor vehicles. The real adventure begins at the end of the trail on Crowell Road.

The bike trail through town is well marked and provides even the novice biker an opportunity to experience breathtaking views like Stage Harbor, the Lighthouse and Morris Island. When you bike in Chatham you experience the lifestyle of a seaside community with endless vistas and horizons. You can take your time and stop to admire gardens full of beautiful perennials, white picket fences, fishing boats and people clamming on the flats. Albert Einstein summed it up. "Life is like riding a bicycle. To keep your balance, you must keep moving."

~Rita Broman

Casseroles & Vegetables

BAKED FRESH CORN

Ingredients:
- 3 tablespoons butter
- 3 tablespoons flour
- 1½ teaspoons salt
- Dash of freshly ground pepper
- 1½ cup light cream
- 2¼ cup cooked corn cut from the cob (8-9 medium ears)
- 3 beaten eggs
- ¾ cup buttered crumbs
- Paprika

Steps:
- Preheat oven to 350°
- Heat butter in a saucepan
- Add flour and blend with a wire whisk.
- Season with salt and pepper
- Meanwhile, bring the cream to a boil and add all at once to the butter flour mixture, stirring vigorously with the whisk until the sauce is thick and smooth
- Remove from the heat and add the corn.
- Slowly add the beaten eggs, stirring constantly
- Pour the mixture into a greased five to six cup casserole.
- Top with the crumbs
- Sprinkle with paprika and place in a shallow pan of hot water
- Bake 45–50 minutes

Serves: 6

What a wonderful vegetable dish. Almost like a soufflé.
~Betsey Stevens

Paddle Tennis

Nestled in the trees on an isolated beach where Pleasant Bay hugs Chatham's shoreline are three Platform Tennis Courts where the Chatham Platform Tennis Association (CPTA) resides. This activity helps the members keep their "wits about them" during the cold and often inclement weather of the fall and winter seasons. The camaraderie of the young and old members is unique. Whether they are experienced or not, everyone gets to play this game called Paddle Tennis.

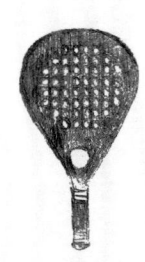

The CPTA organizes Friday night and Sunday Scrambles, Clinics and Round Robins. Most of the members set up their own friendly matches throughout the season from October to April. This special club has existed since the mid-70s when a group of Eastward Ho! avid paddle tennis players convinced the golf course to rent it to their newly formed independent club. It has been managed well since then as the membership has grown to over 250 members.

The courts remind you of downsized tennis courts. However, these have extruded aluminum planking with an abrasive surface which is heated to melt the snow. Heavy chicken wire to the height of 12 feet keeps stray balls in the court. You only get one serve so you better charge the net to win the point. However, if you're receiving, be sure to stay back behind the baseline to return the ball. The balls are smaller than tennis balls and larger than racquet balls but harder than both with a rubber surface. The racquet reminds you of a large table tennis racquet with a very gritty surface which makes it easier to place the ball to win the point.

There is a small building affectionately known as the "Warming Hut" for shelter and relief from the cold. Be prepared to wear several layers of clothing which you will very quickly be removing as your match heats up!!

~Diane Karel

VEGETABLE STEW

Ingredients:
- Large onion cut into half rings
- Olive oil to sauté
- 3 to 4 garlic cloves
- 1 medium eggplant
- 2 (14 ounce) cans of diced tomatoes, fresh if you have them
- Basil, Oregano
- Salt and pepper, to taste
- 1 – 2 zucchini, cut into small pieces
- 1 summer squash, cut into small pieces
- 1 (14 ounce) can chick peas

Steps:
- Lightly brown onion in olive oil
- Add 3-4 garlic cloves cut in small pieces to onions
- Peel and cut eggplant into bite size pieces and add to onion mixture
- Add tomatoes
- Add basil, oregano and ground pepper to taste
- Gently cook until eggplant begins to soften
- Add zucchini, summer squash and chick peas
- Salt to taste
- Simmer mixture until vegetables are soft but not mushy

Note: We serve over polenta but rice also works

This is a good use of summer vegetables in the garden and is also perfect when vegetarians come to dinner.
~Sharon Oudemool

Chatham Baseball

For more than half a century, watching the Chatham baseball team has been a big part of summer fun.

We have always enjoyed Chatham A's baseball games, but 1995 was a special baseball year for our family. We were very proud when our nephew was selected as one of the pitchers for the team. He went to school in a southern state so we hadn't been able to see him play much. During that summer of '95, we were able to see him play a lot! Our extended family formed a cheering section at home games and traveled throughout the Cape to see him pitch. In our minds, we can still see him waving to the crowd from the July 4th float and signing autographs for young fans before a game. We shared the excitement of the whole town when Chatham won their division.

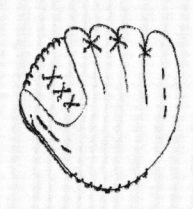

~Deborah Clark & Sue Simpson

EASY CREAMY MACARONI & CHEESE

Ingredients:
- 3 tablespoons butter
- 1 cup cottage cheese (not low-fat)
- 2 cups whole milk (not skim)
- ½ cup sour cream (not low-fat)
- 1 teaspoon dry mustard
- ⅛ teaspoon cayenne pepper
- ⅛ teaspoon nutmeg
- ½ teaspoon salt
- ¼ teaspoon pepper
- 1 pound sharp or extra sharp cheddar cheese, grated
- ½ pound elbow pasta, not cooked
- 1 cup plain breadcrumbs

Steps:
- Heat oven to 375°. Position oven rack in upper ⅓ of oven
- Use 1 tablespoon butter to butter a 9" round or square pan
- In blender puree cottage cheese, milk, sour cream, mustard, cayenne, nutmeg, salt and pepper together
- Reserve ¼ cup grated cheddar cheese for topping
- In large bowl combine remaining grated cheese, milk mixture and uncooked pasta
- Pour into prepared pan. Cover tightly with foil. Bake 45 minutes. Uncover pan
- Stir gently and sprinkle top with reserved cheese and bread crumbs
- Dot with the remaining butter. Bake uncovered for 30-40 minutes until browned
- Let cool at least 15 minutes before serving

~Peggy Sullivan Crespo

RED CABBAGE WITH APPLES

Ingredients:
- 1 medium head red cabbage
- 2 tablespoons chicken fat
- 3 cups water
- ⅔ cup sugar
- ¼ teaspoon pepper
- 1 bay leaf
- 2 or 3 tablespoons flour
- 2 tart apples
- 1 medium onion, sliced
- ⅔ cup red wine vinegar
- ½ teaspoon salt
- 2 whole cloves
- Juice of ½ lemon

Steps:
- Wash cabbage, core, drain and cut as for coleslaw
- Heat chicken fat in a large pot
- Sauté the apples and onions for 3 to 4 minutes
- Add water, vinegar, sugar, salt, pepper, cloves, bay leaf and lemon juice
- Stir and bring to a boil
- Add the cabbage and simmer for 45 minutes, or until tender stirring occasionally
- Just before serving, sprinkle flour on top to absorb some of the liquid

I use my mother-in-law's recipe for red cabbage which is decades old.
~Barbara Schweizer

Seaside Links

Nine holes with mostly hilly narrow fairways and several beautiful ocean views describes Chatham's public course. Located next to Chatham Bars Inn there are no par fives and it is a links course. No call in for tee times; you wait your turn to tee off – but, before you do, wait to see the green disc nearby giving you the all clear signal of the players over the hill. It's a good place to golf for those who are a little over the hill but also a great course to take the grandchildren after a few lessons at a driving range.

It is open year round. If you are not a member, there is a mail slot for your five dollars off season. During the season there are carts as some do describe this as a mountain goat course. No mountain goats to be seen, but foxes, owls and turkeys are not uncommon as well as, unfortunately, the ubiquitous geese. This is a wonderful part of Chatham and enjoyed by many residents several times a week.

~Joanne Donoghue

Crafty Chics

One sunny morning in May of 2006, six women sat around a dining room table creating polymer clay buttons to use on knitted garments. It was great fun crafting and chatting (and chatting) and they wanted to meet again. So began the Crafty Chics of Chatham. More than 100 women have joined the ranks of what has proven to be a collection of talented, creative, crafty-spirited gals. We have shared ideas, suppliers, techniques and stories and have taught each other how to complete a project. Over the years we have done pottery, mosaics, knitting, felting, jewelry, yard ornaments, friendship scarves, basket weaving, polymer clay jewelry, beading, card making, hand-made paper, artist books, ornamental pumpkins, paper beads, crocheted wire and many other items using recyclables as our materials. We have donated fleece blankets to senior citizens and have an on-going baby blanket project for donations to a children's hospital. Our home at the Chatham Community Center is always full of inspiration, humor, information and creative talents being shared.

~Gail Tilton

Cape Cod Weddings

Chatham has become a popular wedding destination. My husband and I have been honored to host two wonderful weddings at our home.

My son and his wife chose Chatham for their destination wedding over five years ago. My niece and her husband decided on a Cape Cod wedding a few years later. Both weddings were festive, happy occasions with sunny skies and perfect weather. Both ceremonies took place in the garden area with a large marquee tent adjacent for the dinner and dancing. Both brides were happy and beautiful and both grooms were dashing. But after that, each couple had their own vision for their perfect day.

One wedding took place in late June with wildflowers blooming, a brass quintet playing music arranged by the bride and energetic, fun swing dancing following a delicious meal. The second wedding was in September with mums and Montauk Daisies in full bloom. Lawn games including ladder golf, a giant KerPlunk game and mini golf followed the ceremony and continued into the evening.

At night both couples concluded the festivities with marshmallow toasting at the fire pit with close friends gathered round. Both couples now look back fondly at their special day. And both events made wonderful memories for our entire family!

~Deborah Clark

CELEBRATIONS

Hooked Rug by Gail Tilton

Desserts

A Chatham Treasure...the Quahog

From the moment my feet hit the sands of Chatham, I couldn't wait to begin my summer career of clamming. My first experience was in Nova Scotia and I carried that love here along with my rake and basket. In 2009 as my daughter planned her wedding on Stage Harbor I knew that clams would have to be a key player in that celebration. A pre-wedding party, called the Clam-o-rama, would be staged at the water's edge overlooking the Stage Harbor Lighthouse.

In the months leading up to the wedding I spent many hours in the company of the gulls and quiet waters of the harbor digging that Chatham treasure.... the quahog. I froze the clam meat and researched my collection of Clam-o-rama recipes that numbered in the dozens. I saved pieces of the beautiful purple wampum that lined the shells of these clams and created pieces of jewelry for each of the bridesmaids. Unexpectedly, that became a summer sideline business at some local craft shows.

Two of the absolute favorite recipes of that beautiful day overlooking Stage Harbor were the Stage Harbor Clam Stew and our Stage Harbor Clams and Sausage in Parsley Sauce and, of course, the drink of the day was the Bog Fog Cranberry Cape Codder .

~Gail Tilton

CELEBRATION COOKIES

Ingredients:
- 1 cup sugar
- ½ cup butter
- 1 egg
- ½ cup sour milk (1½ teaspoon white vinegar stirred into milk, let sit 15 min)
- 2½ cup flour, sifted 3 times
- 1 teaspoon baking powder
- ¼ teaspoon salt
- ½ teaspoon nutmeg
- ½ teaspoon baking soda
- 1 teaspoon anise extract

Icing:
- Confectioners sugar
- Milk

Steps:
- Beat egg, sugar and butter
- Add dry ingredients alternately with milk and extract, beginning and ending with dry
- Roll rounded teaspoon of dough into balls and place on greased cookie sheets
- Bake 375° for about 12 minutes (slightly brown on bottom only)
- Cool on racks
- Mix confectioners sugar and milk to make icing
- Spoon icing over each cookie
- Top with colored sprinkles or nonpareils to suit your celebration
- Let set on waxed paper until dry

~Rose Marie McLoughlin

4th of July Parade

In Chatham it is hip, hip hooray
For the 4th of July parade day

Warm sea breezes and hopefully sun
With many varieties of fun

Red, white and blue banners abound
As musical instruments sound

Clowns, pirates, floats, bands and more
Travel Main Street for us to adore

Hear ye, hear ye, come one, come all
Spectators everywhere have a ball!

~Stephanie Hamilton

Desserts

POTATO CHIP COOKIES

Ingredients:
- 1 pound butter
- 1 cup sugar
- 3 cups flour
- 2 teaspoons vanilla
- 2 cups ruffled potato chips (put in zip top plastic bag and crush by hand)
- Powdered sugar

Steps:
- Cream softened butter and sugar. Add flour and vanilla
- Fold in potato chips with a spoon
- Drop by teaspoon full on an ungreased cookie sheet
- Bake at 350° for 15 minutes
- Sprinkle with powdered sugar

These freeze well!
~Kathie Curran

July 4th Parade

When I was a 12 year old at Camp Avalon, I marched in my first Chatham July 4th parade. Since that time I have sat on the curb at the corner of Main and Shore with my young children holding balloons, watching the early morning floats go by on trailers from our rental on Stage Harbor Road and, more recently, gotten up at five in the morning to put our chairs in the perfect spot. I even marched again - this time with First Night.

For over 50 years the Chatham July 4th parade has been part of my summer. The town fills and we give thanks for good weather. At 9:30 when the police motorcycle announces the parade is coming, my excitement and curiosity are peaked. The parade has changed over the years. No longer do the fishermen and the staff of the Squire have water fights in front of the Squire. Now the politicians march at the back of the parade. And if you were there, how could you forget the protest against abortion? No longer can marchers make a political statement. I wait for the Cobb Family who only march every 5 years because they are so clever. Chatham's 300th Anniversary Parade was special. A tightly timed, no gaps, tribute by residents and groups to Chatham's 300 years. Chatham's July 4th Parade is a very big, small town parade.

~Ann Hosmer

128 *Desserts*

Chocolate Dipped Coconut Macaroons

Ingredients:
- 2⅔ cups flaked coconut, firmly packed
- ⅔ cup sugar
- ¼ cup unbleached flour
- 4 egg whites, unbeaten
- 1 cup sliced almonds
- 1 teaspoon vanilla extract
- 1 teaspoon almond extract
- 8 ounces semi-sweet chocolate morsels, coarsely chopped
- 1 teaspoon butter

Steps:
- Preheat oven to 325°
- Combine coconut, sugar and flour
- Stir in egg whites, almonds, vanilla and almond extract
- Form balls from rounded tablespoons
- Place 2 inches apart on lightly greased cookie sheets
- Bake 20-25 minutes until golden
- Remove from pans while hot and allow to cool
- Makes approximately 30 cookies

Chocolate edge:
- Melt chocolate in double boiler, stirring until ⅔ melted
- Add butter
- Remove from heat and continue stirring until melted
- Dip one edge of each cookie into chocolate and set on wax paper

~Peggy Holtman

Parade Playhouse

My vintage garden shed has many years of family history. It began its colorful life 55 years ago when my father had the notion to have a playhouse built DURING the course of the 4th of July parade in Chatham. This may seem unimaginable, but back then the parade went at a much slower pace and, more or less, meandered down Main Street. My father thought this would be a catchy advertisement for his real estate business and hired a local and prominent Chatham builder. With a small crew working on a trailer towed by a truck, the playhouse was built from scratch on the parade route. Approximately 8 feet by 10 feet, the finished product included bunk beds and four working windows complete with screens.

My younger sister and I spent our early years enjoying our playhouse and perfecting mud cakes. Our childhood playhouse morphed into a teenager's private space ideally suited for sharing secrets and experimentation. As years passed, it was converted from our "hippie" den to a more civilized safe haven with matching curtains and sleeping bags. When my parents decided to sell our family home, I was determined that the playhouse would remain within the family. So my husband and I moved it to our first home on Old Academy Road. With great pleasure, we watched as our two young children enjoyed their grandfather's 4th of July project.

As time moved on, so did we to a new house on Old Harbor Road. Once again, we agreed it must move with us. What used to be my favorite hideaway, safe haven and secret meeting place now stands tall among the lilacs and linden tree in a beautiful perennial garden and continues to hold the things most dear to me. I often wonder, "Is this its final destination?"

~Abigail Doherty

CARROT COOKIES

Ingredients:
- ¾ cup sugar
- ¾ cup shortening
- 1 cup cooked, mashed carrots
- 2 cup flour mixed with 2 t baking powder

Icing:
- ¼ cup orange juice
- 1-3 tablespoon grated orange rind
- 3 tablespoon margarine
- Confectioners sugar

Steps:
- Cream sugar and shortening together
- Add remaining ingredients
- Drop by teaspoonful on an ungreased cookie sheet
- Bake at 375° for 10-12 minutes

Icing steps:
- Melt margarine, add orange juice and grated rind
- Add approximately 2 cups of confectioners sugar until icing is spreading consistency
- After cookie has cooled a little, dip top of cookie in frosting mix

My mother and sister's favorite cookie. The carrots replace eggs and because of a family egg allergy this was an excellent option - and it is delicious!
Deborah Clark

MOLASSES SPICE COOKIES

Ingredients:
- 2¼ cups flour
- 1 teaspoon baking soda
- ¼ teaspoon salt
- 2 teaspoons cinnamon
- 1½ teaspoons ground cloves
- ½ teaspoon ground ginger
- ½ teaspoon ground nutmeg
- 1 cup sugar
- ¾ cup canola oil
- ⅓ cup molasses
- 1 egg
- Extra sugar (for sprinkling)

Steps:
- Preheat oven to 350°
- Line 2 baking sheets with parchment paper
- In a bowl, combine (do not sift) the flour, baking soda, salt, cinnamon, cloves, ginger and nutmeg. Stir well to blend
- In a bowl of an electric mixer, combine the sugar, oil and molasses. Mix on medium low speed for 5 minutes (the mixture looks separated)
- With the mixer running, add the egg and beat for 1 minute
- Turn the mixer to its lowest speed and beat in the dry ingredients in parts, beating each addition thoroughly before adding another. After all of the flour mixture has been added, beat the dough for a few seconds on medium-high speed
- Using 2 soup spoons, drop heaping mounds of dough onto the prepared sheets, leaving 2 inches between them. Use a long metal spatula to lightly press the cookies into rounds about 2" in diameter. You can also roll the dough in your palms and flatten them with the heel of your hand. Place 12 cookies on each sheet
- Sprinkle the tops with sugar and place the baking sheets in the center of the oven. Bake the cookies for 12 – 15 minutes or until they crack on top and are golden. Switch the positions of the baking sheets from back to front halfway through baking
- Remove the cookies from the oven and let them sit for a few minutes. Transfer them to wire racks to cool completely
- Bake the remaining batter

~Ruth Tichenor

Pumpkins in the Park

Autumn is a wonderful time of year in Chatham. You know October has arrived when you enter town and hundreds of pumpkins are on the lawn of the First Congregational Church. The town is less frenzied than during the busy summer months, the weather is brisk but usually sunny and the Pumpkin People appear in Kate Gould Park.

This Chatham tradition gives merchants and organizations a chance to show their pumpkin creativity by erecting themed pumpkin displays. The ideas portrayed are clever, fun to see and always innovative.

This past year, among the dozens of displays, were a centipede pumpkin eater, some large pumpkin M&Ms, pumpkin ducklings, the Mayflower ship with Pumpkin Pilgrims and a reenactment of the First Night Town Photo done with pumpkin people and a lighthouse! The celebration culminates with Oktoberfest weekend where children can play mini-golf and bob for apples, families can vote for their favorite pumpkin display and everyone can enjoy the good food and cheer available. It feels a bit like stepping into a Norman Rockwell painting!

~Sue Simpson and Deborah Clark

NANTUCKET CRANBERRY PIE

Filling Ingredients:
- Butter, to grease the pie plate
- 2 cups fresh or frozen cranberries (or more)
- ½ cup sugar
- ½ cup walnuts, chopped

Topping Ingredients:
- 2 eggs
- ¾ cup butter, softened
- 1 cup sugar
- 1 cup flour
- 1 teaspoon almond extract
- Whipped cream

Filling Steps:
- Preheat the oven to 350°
- Place the cranberries in a buttered, 10" pie plate
- Toss the sugar and walnuts over the berries

For the topping:
- Cream the eggs and the butter with the sugar
- Add the flour and almond extract to the mixture, lightly tossing with a fork
- Put the topping over the cranberry mixture and bake for 35 – 40 minutes
- Flip pie onto serving plate. Serve warm with whipped cream

This is delicious at Thanksgiving and the morning after! It is very pretty served upside down with vanilla ice cream.
~Linda Smith

EASY SWEDISH APPLE PIE

Ingredients:
- 4-6 apples
- cinnamon
- 1 cup sugar
- 1 egg
- 1 cup flour
- 1½ sticks butter, melted
- ½ cup walnuts (optional)

Steps:
- Peel and slice apples and fill a 9" ungreased pie plate ¼ full
- Sprinkle cinnamon over slices

Topping:
- Mix sugar, egg, flour, butter and walnuts
- Place mixture on top of apples covering the apples
- Mixture is a little thick
- Bake at 350° for 40-45 minutes or until crunchy on top

Quick and easy. Super delicious and freezes well.
~Ruth Tichenor

PUMPKIN (OR SQUASH) PIE

Ingredients:
- 1 (15 ounce) can of One-Pie Pumpkin or Squash
- 1 cup brown sugar
- 2 eggs
- 1 cup light cream
- 1 teaspoon cinnamon
- ¼ teaspoon ginger
- ¼ teaspoon nutmeg
- 9 inch pie crust

Steps:
- Preheat oven to 400°
- Mix all ingredients together in a blender
- Pour into a pastry-lined 9" pie plate
- Bake in the 400° oven until the crust is brown
- Reduce the heat to 325° and bake until the filling is firm in the middle, about 40 minutes
- Serve with whipped cream

I asked my husband's aunt for this recipe when we were first married. It is a family Thanksgiving favorite and so easy!
~Ann Hosmer

NUTCRACKER SUITE PIE

Ingredients:
- 3 egg whites
- 1 cup sugar
- ½ teaspoon baking powder
- 1 cup heavy cream, whipped
- ⅔ cup finely chopped nuts
- 14 Ritz crackers, crushed
- ½ teaspoon vanilla or almond extract

Steps:
- Beat eggs, baking powder and vanilla (or almond extract) until fairly stiff
- Add sugar gradually and beat until mixture hold its shape
- Fold in nuts and cracker crumbs
- Put into a well-greased 9" pie plate
- Bake 35 minutes at 325°
- Serve with whipped cream on top
- Put cream on a few hours before serving to mellow flavor

Variations:
- Add 1 square of grated unsweetened or semi-sweet chocolate to mixture before baking
- Cover top of cooked pie with any flavor ice cream and store in freezer. When serving, add any fruit or syrup topping you want with each piece
- Add sliced unsweetened fresh strawberries to pie top before adding whipped cream (favorite variation)

This is one of my favorite family recipes. Great with strawberries.
~Fran Monroe

Chatham Community Center

It was September 6, 1955 when I entered the building for the first time. At that time it was the Chatham School, grades 4-12. I was the newly hired girls physical education teacher and was welcomed by Richard Batchelder, who was a high school teacher and president of the local teachers association. Little did I know that in a few short months I would become his bride.

My assignment was to teach physical education to Grades K-3 in the building on the hill and grades 7-12 in the main building. Additionally, I was to coach the cheerleaders, girls field hockey, girls basketball and girls softball. At the last minute, I was assigned to teach grade 7 math! I did all this for an annual beginning salary of $3,200 a year, which, at the time, was the highest salary level for a beginning teacher in New England.

When I now attend functions at the Chatham Community Center, I reminisce as I sit in the area of what was at one time my classroom. I remember weeping as I watched the rear end of the building being demolished. It housed the gymnasium where my first job was as well as other classrooms where I taught. If you have ever noticed the huge evergreen tree outside the front left side of the building, my class planted it; a Park Ranger insisted it was a good place to plant an 8 inch tree seedling.

~Martha Batchelder

APPLESAUCE CAKE

Ingredients for cake:
    1 cup sugar
    ¼ cup butter or shortening
    1 cup applesauce
    1 teaspoon baking soda
    1½ cup flour
    1 teaspoon cinnamon
    1 teaspoon cloves
    1 teaspoon nutmeg
    1 cup raisins

Ingredients for Icing:
    5 tablespoons brown sugar
    3 tablespoons cream
    2 tablespoons butter
    1-2 cups confectioners sugar
    1 teaspoon vanilla

Steps:
- Mix cake ingredients & bake in lightly greased loaf pan at 325°degrees for 50 minutes
- Test by poking with a knife (time can vary)
- For icing, heat brown sugar, cream and butter. Beat a few minutes and then add vanilla
- Add confectioners sugar as needed to make frosting a smooth consistency
- After cake has cooled, remove from pan and frost top allowing a little to drip over the sides

A favorite recipe for our family from my Great Aunt Edith.
~Deborah Clark

DUNDEE CAKE
NOT YOUR TYPICAL FRUIT CAKE

My mother began making this cake in the 1940s.
~Liz Schmid Hines

Ingredients:
    1 pound butter
    2 cups sugar
    6 eggs
    4 cups cake flour
    1 teaspoon salt
    ½ teaspoon mace
    1 pound shelled, chopped walnuts
    1 pound raisins, floured
    3 (8 ounce) jars maraschino cherries, drained
    Splash of premium brandy

Steps:
- Preheat oven to 325°
- Cream butter and sugar.
- Add eggs one at a time
- Sift dry ingredients together
- Add to mixture
- Add walnuts, raisins and cherries
- Add a good splash of premium brandy
- Bake at 325° for 2 hours in two lightly greased 9 x 5 x 3 inch bread pans (do not use another type of pan)
- When done, turn onto wire rack to cool

Note: This cake can be frozen. Because it's so rich, it can be sliced frozen

SUGAR COOKIE POUND CAKE

Ingredients:
- 3 cups sugar cookie crumbs, either homemade or store-brought such as Pepperidge Farm Chessman cookie
- 2 cups sliced almonds, coarsely ground
- 1 cup unsalted butter, softened
- 2 cups sugar
- 6 eggs
- ½ cup flour
- ½ cup half and half
- 1 tablespoon vanilla extract
- 2 teaspoons almond extract
- 3 tablespoons confectioners sugar for dusting finished cake

Steps:
- Preheat oven to 300°
- Crush sugar cookies to a fine crumb-like texture
- Grind almonds with a chef's knife or food processor
- Put softened butter in mixer and gradually add sugar
- Add eggs one at a time until thoroughly incorporated
- Stir until mixture has no lumps
- In separate bowl, mix flour and sugar cookie crumbs
- Put mixer on low speed, then add cookie crumb mixture and the half and half alternately
- Add extracts and continue to mix
- Add almonds last, mixing in thoroughly being careful not to over-beat
- Use a Bundt or tube pan. Cut parchment paper to fit the bottom of the pan and place inside
- Grease pan and parchment paper and flour heavily (this cake does not rise a lot)
- Bake for 2 hours
- Remove and cool in the pan on a wire rack
- When cooled peel away parchment paper and dust heavily with confectioners sugar

~Peggy Sullivan Crespo

Favorite Family Cheesecake

Crust Ingredients:
- 1¼ cup graham crackers (about 8-9 crackers)
- ¼ cup melted butter
- ¼ cup sugar

Filling Ingredients:
- 4 (8 ounce) packages cream cheese
- 6 eggs
- 1 cup sugar
- 1½ teaspoons vanilla

Topping Ingredients:
- 2 cups sour cream
- ¼ cup sugar
- 1 teaspoon vanilla

Steps:
- Crust: Using the food processor, process the crackers into fine crumbs. Blend the crust ingredients until evenly moistened. Spread in a buttered 9 inch springform pan, covering sides and bottom. Chill until needed
- Filling: Preheat oven to 375°. Combine filling ingredients gradually in processor. Blend until smooth (1-2 minutes). Pour into chilled crust; spread evenly. Bake for 40 minutes. Remove from oven and cool for 30 minutes. Reset oven to 475°
- Topping: Prepare topping by blending topping ingredients with spoon. Spread over cool filling. Return to oven for 5 minutes. Cool at room temperature for 6 hours to allow center to set.
- Do not attempt to cut before that length of time has expired.
- Refrigerate and serve

Serves 16

A very smooth and luscious cheesecake. I've tried a lot of cheesecake but I always come back to this one. Use of a food processor is the trick to making it super smooth!

~Sue Simpson

FESTIVE CRANBERRY TORTE

Ingredients:
- 1½ cups graham cracker crumbs
- ½ cup chopped pecans
- 1¼ cups sugar
- 6 tablespoons butter, melted
- 1½ cups fresh, ground cranberries (or 2 cups whole)
- 2 egg whites, unbeaten
- 1 tablespoon frozen orange juice concentrate, thawed
- 1 teaspoon vanilla
- ⅛ teaspoon salt
- 1 cup whipping cream
- Fresh orange slices, quartered

Cranberry Glaze:
- ½ cup sugar
- 1 tablespoon cornstarch
- ¾ cup fresh cranberries
- ⅔ cup water

Steps:
- Combine graham cracker crumbs, pecans, ¼ cup sugar and melted butter
- Press into bottom and up side of 8" spring form pan. Chill
- Combine cranberries and 1 cup sugar. Let stand for 5 minutes
- Add unbeaten egg whites, orange juice concentrate, vanilla and salt to cranberry mixture
- Beat on low speed in electric mixer until frothy, about 6 - 8 minutes or until it forms stiff peaks
- In small bowl whip cream to soft peaks. Fold into cranberry mixture
- Turn into crust. Freeze until firm
- Place on serving dish. Spoon glaze in center
- Decorate with orange slices

Cranberry Glaze:
- In sauce pan, stir together sugar and cornstarch
- Stir in cranberries and water. Cook and stir until bubbly
- Continue stirring until cranberry skins pop
- Cool to room temp (do not chill)
- Makes 2 cups

In loving memory of my sister, Susan Joan Schmid
~Liz Schmid Hines

First Night Chatham

From the town photo at noon until the final fireworks at midnight, Chatham is the place to be on New Year's Eve. If the temperature was not freezing, you might think it was a summer day. The police estimate at least 10,000 visitors fill the town, a huge number when you think that in 1991 two Chatham women got together to plan the original Chatham First Night. A family friendly, alcohol free celebration of the arts, First Night now offers over 70 performances at churches, schools, the community center, town hall and the new Orpheum Theater. This self-supporting day and night is organized and run by a committee of volunteers. With two firework shows, a noise parade, the countdown cod, a circus, crafts for kids, music of all kinds, (big band, klezmer, barbershop, piano, jazz), dancing, magic shows, wood and ice carving, a horse and buggy ride, a fabulous train display and a road race led by a gorilla, the cost of a button is a real bargain. Buy your button early online or in person because the 7,500 buttons sell out.

~Ann Hosmer

DESSERT SURPRISE

Ingredients:
- 17 ice cream sandwiches or so –depends on size of dish and size of sandwiches
- 1 (12.25 ounce) jar caramel topping (or similar)
- 1¼ cup chopped pecans
- 1 (12 ounce) Cool Whip, thawed. Buy small size also just in case
- ¾ cup hot fudge topping

Steps:
- Place 8½ sandwiches (or enough to cover the bottom) in 9 x 13 inch Pyrex pan or the like
- Spread evenly with caramel topping
- Sprinkle with 1 cup pecans
- Top with 2 cups of Cool Whip to cover
- Place remaining sandwiches on top
- Spread remaining Cool Whip to cover
- Sprinkle with remaining pecans
- Cover
- Freeze for at least 2 hours. Can be frozen overnight or more
- Remove from freezer
- Let stand 5 minutes or so to soften a little
- Cut into squares
- Heat hot fudge topping
- Drizzle over squares

What a surprise this dessert is when you see how it is made. Delicious!
~Susan Turner Pinzuti

Harvest Pear Crisp with Candied Ginger

Topping Ingredients:
- ½ cup all-purpose flour
- ½ cup packed dark brown sugar
- ½ teaspoon ground cinnamon
- ¼ teaspoon sea salt
- ½ cup (1 stick) chilled unsalted butter, cut into ½ inch cubes
- 1 cup old-fashioned oats
- ½ cup coarsely chopped whole raw almonds
- ¼ cup of ¼ inch cubes crystallized ginger

Filling Ingredients:
- ½ cup sugar
- 2 tablespoons cornstarch
- ½ teaspoon ground cinnamon
- ¼ teaspoon sea salt (or Kosher salt)
- 4 pounds firm but ripe pears (6 to 7 large), peeled, cored, cut into ½ inch cubes (about 6 cups)

Topping Steps:
- Whisk first 4 ingredients in medium bowl
- Add butter. Working quickly so butter does not soften, rub in with fingertips until moist clumps form
- Stir in oats, almonds and ginger
- Cover and chill while preparing filling
- Can be made one day ahead.

Filling Steps:
- Preheat oven to 350°
- Whisk first 4 ingredients in large bowl
- Add pears, toss. Transfer to 13 x 9 inch baking dish
- Sprinkle topping over pear mixture
- Bake until topping is crisp golden brown and juices are bubbling, about 50 minutes

Serve warm

Originally I served this crisp on Thanksgiving for those who did not want pie. My family now eats all of the crisp then the pies!

~Mary Melo

LISA DERY'S BERRY BUCKLE

Topping Ingredients:
- ½ cup sugar
- ½ teaspoon cinnamon
- ¼ teaspoon nutmeg
- ⅓ cup flour
- ¼ cup butter, chilled

Cake Ingredients:
- ¾ cup sugar
- ¼ cup Crisco
- 1 egg
- 1 cup milk
- 2 cups flour (save 1 tablespoon to toss with berries)
- ½ teaspoon salt
- 2 teaspoons baking powder
- 1 cup fresh/frozen cranberries
- 1 cup blueberries

Topping Steps:
- Cut up butter and cut into dry ingredients
- Set aside

Cake Steps:
- Preheat oven 350°
- Using electric mixer, cream sugar and Crisco
- Add egg and beat well
- Add dry ingredients alternating with milk
- Fold in 2 cups of berries tossed with the 1 tablespoon flour
- Spread in buttered 9 x 12 inch pan and spoon topping to cover the batter
- Bake at 350° for 45-50 minutes

This old-fashioned dessert/coffee cake is easy and delicious with any combination of berries. Hint: make topping the night before and refrigerate.

~Alayne Tsigas

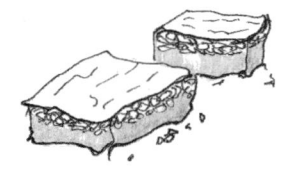

Remembering Veterans

So proud to be an American and to stand tall
We march to the beat of this celebratory call
In the special parades for our veterans
(Chatham's Memorial Day and Veterans Day) we bear it all
So proud to live in a town where honor is paid
For those who served to keep us free and the groundwork was laid
So proud we live free because so many do not
In this beautiful town by the sea which is a very special spot.

~Jo Ann Sprague

CRANBERRY~APPLE CASSEROLE

Ingredients:
- 3 cups chopped uncooked, peeled apples
- 2 cups uncooked cranberries
- ¾ cup sugar
- 1 cup oats
- ⅓ cup butter, melted
- ⅓ cup all-purpose flour
- ½ cup brown sugar
- ½ cup chopped nuts

Steps:
- Put apples and cranberries in 2 quart casserole
- Sprinkle with sugar
- In a bowl, combine oats, butter, flour, brown sugar and nuts
- Spread over the fruit
- Bake at 350° for 1 hour

Note: Can serve with vanilla ice cream if desired
Serves 8

This delicious dessert uses New England apples and Cape Cod cranberries

~Edie Ward

INDIAN PUDDING

Ingredients:
- 3 cups milk
- ½ cup molasses
- ⅓ cup yellow cornmeal
- ½ teaspoon ginger
- ½ teaspoon ground cinnamon
- 1 tablespoon butter
- ¼ teaspoon salt

Steps:
- In a saucepan, mix milk and molasses
- Stir in cornmeal, ginger, cinnamon and salt
- Cook and stir until thick, about 10 minutes
  - Stir in butter
  - Turn into 1 quart casserole
  - Bake uncovered at 300° about 1 hour

Note: Best served hot with vanilla ice cream on top!
Serves 6

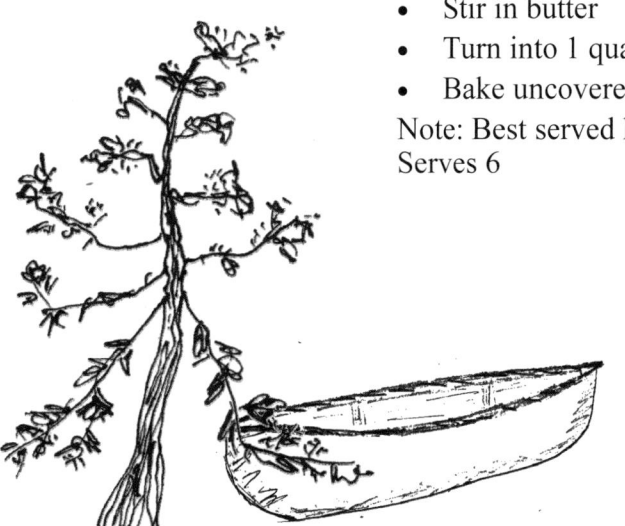

Indian pudding is a traditional New England dessert and is a fancy form of Hasty Pudding. I grew up loving this when made by my mother from Portland, Maine.

~Jennifer Ukstins

Godfrey's Windmill

Imagine Chatham on a windy day in 1797. You are bringing your wagon full of corn up the hill overlooking Mill Pond and there is Colonel Godfrey's new windmill. The eight-sided mill is an impressive sight, standing thirty feet tall on top of Mill Hill. The arms are covered with sails made of flax grown and woven by a neighbor. You can hear the grinding of the millstones brought from Europe as ballast on a ship returning to Chatham. The cap on the top of the mill looks like an upside down boat. The miller turns the cap using the long-tail pole so the sails catch the wind.

As you visit with your neighbors you hope the newly ground cornmeal will be used to make Indian Pudding for your supper. Godfrey's Mill served the town until 1898. Today it is located in Chase Park and can still grind corn when the wind is just right.

~Jennifer Ukstins

Tiramisu Anacapri

Ingredients:
- 1 cup cold water
- 1 (14 ounce) can sweetened condensed milk
- 1 (14 ounce) package of sugar-free vanilla instant pudding mix
- 1 (8 ounce) package of cream cheese, softened
- 1 (8 ounce) tub of frozen whipped topping thawed
- 1 cup hot water
- ½ cup Kahlua (coffee flavored liqueur)
- 1 heaping tablespoon instant espresso or 2 heaping tablespoons instant coffee granules
- 24 ladyfingers—2 (3 ounce) packages
- 3 tablespoons unsweetened cocoa divided

Steps:
- Combine first 3 ingredients in a large bowl; stir well with a whisk. Cover surface with plastic wrap; chill 30 minutes or until firm
- Remove plastic wrap and add cream cheese. Beat with a mixer at medium speed until well blended and smooth. Gently fold in whipped topping
- Combine hot water, Kahlua and espresso. Split lady fingers in half lengthwise. Arrange 16 ladyfinger halves, flat sides down, in a trifle bowl or large glass bowl. Drizzle with ½ cup liqueur mixture. Spread ⅓ of pudding mixture evenly over lady fingers; sprinkle by sifting 1 tablespoon of cocoa over pudding mixture. Repeat layers, ending with cocoa. Cover and chill at least 6 hours

Serves 10-12

This hasty and tasty tiramisu makes an elegant dessert to serve at a dinner party. Guests will beg you for the recipe.

~Eileen Gibb

BUTTERCRUNCH

Ingredients:
- 2 cups sugar
- 1 pound unsalted butter
- 5 tablespoons water
- 10 ounces milk chocolate, grated
- 1½ cups chopped walnuts or pecans

Steps:
- Evenly sprinkle the bottom of a 9 x 12 inch pan with half the nuts, then half the grated chocolate
- In heavy pan, combine the first 3 ingredients over medium heat.
- When the syrup reaches 285° degrees on the candy thermometer (or a soft crack) take it off the heat and pour it evenly over the chocolate
- Immediately sprinkle the rest of the chocolate evenly over the surface, followed by the rest of the nuts
- Cool to room temperature before cutting or breaking into bite size pieces
- Store the candy in refrigerator, either in the pan covered with foil or in containers after cutting

Note: Use a candy thermometer.
Candy is best made when humidity is low

Buttercrunch was a popular thank you gift for a friend who had taken care of children or helped in other ways. I still make many batches at holiday time for the members of my extended family.
~Barbara Schweizer

Sunday Beach Services

In the summer, from June to Labor Day, if you venture down to Oyster Pond on a Sunday morning at 8:00 a.m. you may hear voices singing. For about ten years, the Chatham Clergy, both active and retired, have offered a variety of Sunday services to those who gather there on the beach sitting on blankets or chairs. There is a boat shaped pulpit built by local woodworkers and flowers in simple vases picked from family gardens. There is something very special about being on the beach with your feet in the sand looking out over the water, watching the birds swoop and glide while listening to words of encouragement and love and maybe even singing a familiar song.

~Gail Smith

The Charms of Chatham
~Appetizers & Beverages~

Appetizers

Artichoke Tarts	19
Baked Stuffed Quahogs	9
Candied Walnut Cranberry Spread	20
Cheese Straws	13
Cranberry Glazed Brie	21
Eggplant Spread	14
Fig & Brie Torte	21
Herb Cheese Stuffed Mushrooms	15
Italian Appetizer Bites	16
Mom's Clam Dip	10
Pear & Almond Croustade	23
Pita Chips	18
Smoked Oyster Paté	11

Beverages

Cape Cod Margarita	25
Dad's Punch	24

Commemoratives
~Soups, Salads & More~

Soups

Chilled Cucumber Soup	30
Clam Bisque	34
Gazpacho	33
Portuguese Kale Soup	37
Scallop Soup	35
Summer Tomato Lemon Soup	29
Vichyssoise	31
Winter Squash & Shrimp Chowder	36

Salads

Broccoli Salad	42
Cauliflower Salad	43
Mandarin Orange Salad	40
Oriental Broccoli Salad	41
Shoepeg Salad	43
Spring~Summer Strawberry Salad	39
Watermelon Salad	39

Breads, Jellies & More

Beach Plum Jelly	47
Blueberry Cake – A Hot Bread	44
Bryan's Favorite Pickles	48
Lemon Blueberry Bread	45

Coastal
~Seafood~

Baked Finnan Haddie	66
Bouillabaisse	54
Broiled Oriental Swordfish	72
Chatham Half Shell Mussels Neopolitan	62
Company Fish	69
Coquilles Saint Jacques	61
Fantastic Fish Pie	58
Fish Stew	57
Honey Mustard Glazed Salmon	70
Mussels Dijon	63
Oysters & Corn Casserole	64
Sea Scallops with Lemon~Butter Sauce	65
Sesame Broiled Salmon with Wasabi Marinade	71
Stage Harbor Clam Stew	53
Swordfish or Tuna ~Olives, Capers, & More~	73
Seafood Cioppino (Stew)	55

Community
~Meats and Poultry~

Asian Orange Chicken	87
Boneless Roast Pork w/ Plum Sauce	100
Brisket & Beans	96
Chicken Chow Mein	86
Chicken Divan	79
Chicken Picatta	80
Chicken Stew	88
Company Chicken	84
Easy, Elegant Turkey & Spinach	92
Golfer's Stew	95
Hot Chicken Salad	91
London Broil	99
Quick Chicken Curry	90
Stuffed Cabbage	94
Veal Milanese	102

Competitions
~Casseroles and Vegetables~
Casseroles

Broccoli Cheese Casserole	115
Carrot Soufflé	117
Cheddar & Sausage Breakfast Casserole	109
Chicken & Noodle Supreme	111
Easy Creamy Macaroni & Cheese	121
Pilgrim Potatoes	112
Reuben Bake	110

Vegetables

Baked Fresh Corn	118
Carrot Pennies	116
Cucumbers with Vinegar, Oil & Parsley	107
Potatoes Romanoff	112
Red Cabbage with Apples	122
Sesame Snow Peas	114
Sweet Potatoes with Pecans & Bourbon	113
Vegetable Stew	120

Celebrations
~Desserts~
Cookies

Carrot Cookies	131
Celebration Cookies	127
Chocolate Dipped Coconut Macaroons	129
Molasses Spice Cookies	132
Potato Chip Cookies	128

Cakes & Pies

Applesauce Cake	138
Dundee Cake	138
Easy Swedish Apple Pie	135
Favorite Family Cheesecake	140
Festive Cranberry Torte	141
Nantucket Cranberry Pie	134
Nutcracker Suite Pie	136
Pumpkin (or Squash) Pie	135
Sugar Cookie Pound Cake	139

Desserts & More

Buttercrunch	149
Cranberry~Apple Casserole	145
Dessert Surprise	142
Harvest Pear Crisp with Candied Ginger	143
Indian Pudding	146
Lisa Dery's Berry Buckle	144
Tiramisu Anacapri	148